D1358687

FOOD ESSENTIALS

POULTRY

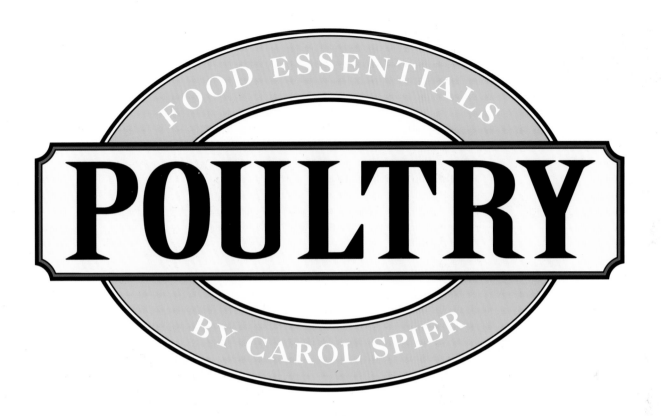

FOOD ESSENTIALS
POULTRY
BY CAROL SPIER

PHOTOGRAPHY BY BILL MILNE

Kathy Blake—Food Stylist

Maxine Kaplan—The Prop Co.

O. Ottomanelli and Sons—Game

CRESCENT BOOKS
NEW YORK • AVENEL, NEW JERSEY

A FRIEDMAN GROUP BOOK

This 1993 edition published by Crescent Books, distributed by Outlet Book Company, Inc., a Random House Company, 40 Engelhard Avenue, Avenel, New Jersey 07001.

Copyright © 1993 by Michael Friedman Publishing Group, Inc.

All rights reserved. No part of this publication may be reproduced, stored in a retrieval system, or transmitted, in any form or by any means, electronic, photocopying, recording, or otherwise, without the prior written permission of the publisher.

ISBN 0-517-06119-8

FOOD ESSENTIALS: POULTRY
was prepared and produced by
Michael Friedman Publishing Group, Inc.
15 West 26th Street
New York, New York 10010

Editors: Nathaniel Marunas and Suzanne DeRouen
Art Director: Jeff Batzli
Photography Editor: Ede Rothaus
Layout: Beverly Bergman
Production: Jeanne E. Kaufman

Typeset by Trufont Typographers, Inc.
Color separations by Rainbow Graphic Arts Co., Ltd.
Printed and bound in Hong Kong by Leefung-Asco Printers Ltd.

8   7   6   5   4   3   2   1

TABLE OF CONTENTS

DEDICATION

For Bruce McCandless, a wonderful photographer and friend who happens to find wild turkey shooting a great sport, and without whose patient explanations I would not have understood the thrill of that activity or the preparation of its bounty. And for the King family at North Sea Farms, in hopes that they will continue to produce the best poultry on the East End, so that my husband and our friends and felines can look forward to many more delightful chickens, capons, Muscovy and Long Island ducklings, and Cornish hens.

ACKNOWLEDGMENTS

I am indebted to the publicists at the National Broiler Council, the National Turkey Federation, and Concord Ducks for information on poultry farming, and to the Wild Turkey Federation for information on the habits and hunting of that bird. Without the good faith and humorous support of Karla Olson, lovely editor, this book would not have happened; many thanks to her and all the hard-workers at Michael Friedman.

PREFACE

There are those people who are natural cooks, and those who quake at the idea of preparing anything more complex than scrambled eggs on toast. The former tend to be creative in the kitchen, and are always on the lookout for both new ideas and basic culinary knowledge that will allow them to follow a whim with a certain guarantee of success; the latter rarely reach beyond the tried-and-true without a cookbook in hand. The former may eschew measuring spoons in favor of "season to taste," while the latter ponder level versus heaping. Both will find guidance and inspiration in the *Food Essentials* series.

Topically organized, these volumes contain the basics of food preparation in an accessible and straightforward format.

But they are much more than convenient, alphabetized indexes of what-is-it-called and how-do-you-cook-it. The *Food Essentials* volumes address all of the culinary needs of today's cook, explaining not only the elemental aspects of buying, storage, and preparation, but the nutritional role played by each of the various foods. The contemporary attitude expressed throughout is one of good health through good food with as little trouble as possible; the diversity of the recipes is unified by common-sense nutrition, fresh ingredients simply but delightfully seasoned, and ease of preparation. The text is sprinkled with bits of food history and countless suggestions for seasoning variations. Both timid and adventurous cooks will be rewarded with every reading of these essential volumes.

Many of us can't get through a week of menu planning without including chicken at least once—and with good reason. It is inexpensive, versatile, easy to prepare, and delicious. And in this era of health-conscious dining when almost everything that tastes good is supposedly "bad" for you, chicken can be eaten without excessive guilt. The same can be said of turkey and, with the exception of the price tag, most of the game birds. Even duck and goose, notoriously fatty fowl, have a legitimate place in contemporary cuisine if properly prepared.

When you decide to cook a bird, there are many choices to make before you come anywhere near the table. First, which bird? Chicken, turkey, duck, goose, or something more exotic—pheasant, guinea fowl, tiny quail, or richly flavored squab? Then, how to cook it? Roasted, grilled, braised, baked, sautéed? What sort of seasoning? With a simple squeeze of lemon juice, in a complex mélange of wine and herbs, or with an indulgence of butter or cream? The choices are myriad and the prospects endless.

Luckily, most poultry is so inexpensive and easy to prepare that you can choose many of these possibilities often. To make matters less confusing, this volume balances the need to present simple, healthful, and appealing recipes with the rich culinary tradition of its subject. The recipes are complemented with practical and basic cooking information that will allow anyone to prepare the birds successfully, but encourage the adventurous to experiment as well. As you browse through the pages, feel free to mix and match seasonings and cooking techniques: Many baked dishes are just as tasty if grilled, and many recipes can be given an entirely different flavor by simply changing the primary herb. Because chicken is the bird most of us prepare most often, more recipes are suggested for it than for the others, but you can—as long as you consider the different cooking requirements—substitute. Chicken is appropriate for so many meals that all the seasoning possibilities are welcome. The more exotic birds, however, are most likely reserved for special occasions; they are wonderfully flavorful on their own and you will never go wrong simply roasting them. Indeed, if you are not familiar with these birds, I recommend roasting to really appreciate their unique tastes. Turkey and duck fall somewhere in between for most of us, so prepare them as your experience and mood dictate.

Before selecting a recipe or heading to the market, let's take a moment to understand the subject at hand. The term *poultry* refers to fowl that are domesticated—bred and raised to grace the table. Poultry raising has been understood and practiced worldwide for thousands of years, but electricity, refrigeration, and scientific breeding technology have enabled it to become a commercial enterprise rather than a homemaker's task. Game birds are by tradition wild fowl, living free and appearing on the table only when a skilled or lucky hunter brings them home. Today, however, many of them are also farmed, often in free-range conditions (semiconfined in their natural habitats or approximations thereof), and are available fresh or frozen year round, so it is no longer necessary to know a hunter to enjoy them. The game birds discussed in this volume are available from specialty markets and a few mail-order sources. It is assumed that the birds you will be preparing are dressed (cleaned and plucked) and ready to cook. Should you be lucky enough to receive birds from a hunter, trust his knowledge about the best cooking technique for the particular specimens. The flavor of all birds is directly affected by their diet and age, and this is particularly true of those that are wild. Age also affects tenderness, so the older a bird is the tougher its meat will be: This is why young birds can be quickly grilled or roasted, while older ones should be slowly simmered. But don't discount older birds—age can also bring rich flavor.

A brief mention should be made about serving size. Current dietary guidelines suggest that a three-ounce portion of boneless, skinless poultry per person is ideal. The portions suggested in this book, however, are a bit more satisfying and gauged for a more traditional appetite. But let experience guide you—you no doubt have cooked enough chicken to know how much your family will eat at one meal. The recipes

for sauces and marinades are generous enough to allow you to cook a bit more bird than indicated without doubling them, but if you increase the quantity of bird substantially, by all means increase the other components of the recipe.

Do explore the availability of the birds that you have rarely or never prepared. Should you live near a good butcher or small poultry farmer who offers goose at holiday time, try it— goose is no more difficult to cook than turkey. Though duck, because of its higher fat content, is not as versatile as chicken, it is just as easy to prepare. Quail and squab are appearing more frequently in grocery freezers, so take a look. Or perhaps the chef at a good local restaurant would be willing to order pheasant for you when he plans to have it on the menu. And chicken, of course, can be enjoyed on any day. Whether you plan ahead and let poultry marinate until it's suffused with seasoning, or simply stick the bird in the oven to roast with a sprinkling of salt and pepper, you will always have a delicious meal.

Chicken is such a frequent and favorite item on our menus that it is surprising to learn that it has been readily available for only the last fifty or sixty years. While rural farmers have raised chickens for their eggs for centuries, their meat was considered dry and uninteresting. Only those hatched in the spring and raised outdoors were brought young to the table, though older hens would find their way to the stew pot when their egg-laying days were over. It was not until the 1930s, when scientists discovered that chickens fed vitamins D and B_{12} could be bred and raised indoors to be tender and juicy year-round, that the treat of a "spring chicken" became a staple of contemporary diet. Today poultry growing is a huge, regulated, and scientific industry, where different kinds of chickens are bred either to produce eggs or to be meaty and tender.

Poultry growing is no longer a small-farm enterprise. A typical poultry company owns or manages all parts of the production process, including feed mill, hatchery, contract growers (who actually raise the chickens once hatched), processing and packaging plant, field service, and management personnel. Most companies maintain research staffs, employ veterinarians, and do their own breeding, shipping, and marketing. Every chicken is inoculated against disease upon hatching and individually hand-inspected before it is packaged. Great care is taken to keep the birds calm and to kill them humanely, if for no other reason than that bruised poultry flesh cannot be sold for human consumption. All facilities are thoroughly cleaned before each processing shift.

Chickens eat primarily corn and soybean meal. They receive vitamin and mineral supplements. They are not given steroids or growth hormones. Some chickens are raised with noticeably yellow flesh. This is a result of a diet rich in corn, alfalfa, or marigold petals and has no effect on nutritional value, flavor, tenderness, or fat content; it is simply that consumers in some regions seem to prefer yellower chickens.

Free-range chickens are allowed unlimited access to the outdoors while they are reaching table weight. The conditions in which they are raised may vary with the region or type or size of grower, but in general they are raised in small flocks on farms where they eat simple mixtures of grains and what they find in the barnyard or field. Because of this it may take longer for a free-range chicken to reach market weight. Aficionados insist that free-range chickens have a better flavor than those raised by large growers, but poultry industry representatives deny that a blind taste-test will reveal any difference in taste or texture.

Chicken is a high-protein, low-calorie meat that provides significant amounts of some vitamins and minerals, including iron and vitamins A, B_1, and B_2; the highest concentration of these is found in the liver. The fat present in poultry is not marbled into the flesh as it is in beef or pork, but is found mostly in or under the skin; removing the skin before or after cooking cuts the fat content nearly in half. Because chickens have been bred to grow quickly, some of their feed may be metabolized as fatty deposits rather than tissue; these are sometimes found in the chest cavities and can be easily cut off before cooking. The breast and wings of chicken are white meat; the thighs and drumsticks are dark meat.

Chicken is one of the most versatile foods in our diet. It is inexpensive, available in many forms, and can be prepared in seemingly endless ways. Inherently flavorful, chicken is delicious simply broiled or baked; it has been incorporated into meat-eating cuisines all around the world and is complemented by almost any seasoning. There are many traditional chicken dishes that are resplendent with rich sauces but contemporary health-conscious cooks will find that herbs, vegetables, and fruits, and perhaps a little wine, provide so many tasty, nutritious, and often easy-to-prepare seasoning possibilities that no one should ever say "chicken . . . again?" with dismay.

Poussin

A poussin is a chicken that is less than four weeks old. Poussins have proportionately larger breasts than older chickens; their flesh is tender and juicy with a delicate flavor. They usually weigh about one pound with a large proportion of flesh to carcass. They are very good grilled, broiled, or roasted. Allow one poussin per serving.

Broilers and Fryers

Broilers and fryers are young chickens of either sex marketed at six to eight weeks of age and weighing between two-and-a-half and four-and-a-half pounds. Traditionally, broilers are smaller than fryers but the poultry industry uses the terms interchangeably today. They have tender flesh, can be prepared just about any way you wish, and are very good grilled, broiled, fried, or roasted. Allow one-quarter to one-half broiler or fryer per serving.

Broilers and fryers are available in many forms in most grocery stores. *Whole birds*, usually accompanied by their giblets, can be cooked as they are or cut up by the consumer; this is usually the least expensive way to buy chicken. *Cut-up chickens* (usually one bird per pack and accompanied by giblets) are either quartered or cut into smaller pieces: two breasts, wings,

thighs, and drumsticks; the back is sometimes separate and sometimes attached to the breast and thighs. Cut-up chicken is usually more expensive than whole chicken. Packages of *chicken parts* include breasts, wings, thighs, or drumsticks, and usually contain four or more of one part of the bird.

The price per pound varies with the cut, with breast being the most expensive. Boneless and skinless breasts are called *supremes*, *cutlets*, or *filets*. Both breasts and thighs are available boneless and usually skinless: These are the most expensive cuts of chicken to buy.

In answer to the growing demand for lower-fat protein, many poultry producers are now offering ground chicken, which can be cooked like ground beef (see *A Word on Ground Chicken and Turkey*, page 95). Packages of *chicken giblets*—hearts, gizzards, and livers—are often sold mixed, and the livers are usually available separately. Many grocers also carry prepared fresh chicken that is ready-to-cook. This may be a seasoned whole bird that is set for the oven or cutlets or nuggets that are breaded and ready to pan fry. *Smoked chicken* is also available in a variety of cuts. Look for it in specialty shops or the gourmet section of the grocery. It is very good in salads and hors d'oeuvres.

Roasters

Roasters are also chickens of either sex. *Young roasters* are specially raised broiler-type chickens weighing between six and eight pounds. Traditional roasters are a little older and weigh between three-and-a-half and five pounds. The flesh of either type is still tender and, as their name implies, they are very good roasted, rotisseried, or cooked in liquid on the stove top. Allow three-quarters to one pound per serving when buying a whole bird (or one-third to one-half pound cutlet per serving).

Fowl

Fowl are hens that are ten months or older. Male chickens of this age are sometimes called stag or cock, but both sexes may be referred to as boilers. *Heavy hens* are mature laying hens from the broiler side of the poultry industry and are plumper than hens who lay eggs for the table. Fowl are too tough to broil or roast and should be cooked in liquid to tenderize; they make excellent soup, stew, or stock.

Capons

Capons are castrated male chickens. They are between ten and twelve months old and weigh eight to nine-and-a-half pounds. They have a greater proportion of white to dark meat than other chickens have and are very tender and

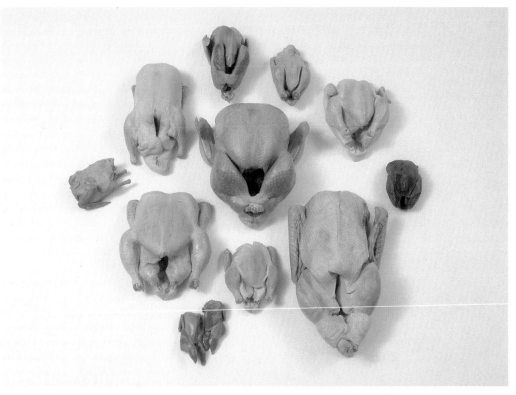

Whole birds: a turkey in the center and, clockwise from lower right, goose, Cornish hen, two quail, capon, partridge, duck, pheasant, guinea fowl, chicken, and grouse.

flavorful. They can be found at specialty poultry shops or local poultry farms, where they may be seasonal. Capon may be cooked just about any way you wish. It is very good roasted (it's a good substitute for turkey when you are feeding six to eight people) and stewed; it also makes rich stock. Capon may be substituted for pheasant or grouse. Allow three-quarters to one pound per serving.

Cornish Game Hens

Cornish game hens are the result of crossbreeding the Cornish gamecock with the Plymouth Rock hen. They are a domesticated fowl and were first developed in the 1950s in the United States. Cornish game hens are five to seven weeks old and weigh between one and two pounds. They may be prepared following any chicken recipe and are usually roasted whole or split and grilled or broiled. Smaller ones may be substituted for poussin, baby pheasant, or squab. Allow one-half to one Cornish game hen (or about one pound) per serving.

HOW TO ROAST A WHOLE CHICKEN, CAPON, OR CORNISH GAME HEN

Refer also to *How to Stuff and Truss a Bird*, page 106, and *How to Roast a Whole Bird*, page 108. Preheat the oven to 450°F. Place the bird in the oven and reduce the temperature to 350°F. Roast chicken for 20 minutes a pound unstuffed, or 25 minutes a pound stuffed. Roast Cornish hens for 30 to 40 minutes. Roast capon for 15 minutes a pound unstuffed, and 20 minutes a pound stuffed, but check early for doneness. Allow a roast chicken or game hen to rest about 10 minutes before carving, and a capon about 15 to 20 minutes.

BONELESS BREASTS AND CUTLETS

The breast meat of chicken is tender, succulent, and versatile. If the breasts are halved, boneless, and skinless (often called *supremes*), they can be easily and quickly prepared in myriad ways; the key to cooking them successfully is not to overcook them. They can be prepared whole or cut into smaller pieces, cut horizontally into two cutlets or filets, cubed for kebabs, or sliced into very small pieces for stir-frying. They can be pounded thin, stuffed, and rolled; sautéed, poached, baked, or broiled; or served plain or with almost any imaginable sauce.

Here are a few guidelines:
To pound to make thin: Place the breasts or cutlets between wax paper and pound with a wooden mallet or side of a rolling pin until desired thickness is reached. If you plan to roll and stuff them, be careful not to pound holes into the flesh. When preparing chicken in this way, remember to cut down on the cooking times; they are done when springy to the touch and when the juices run clear if a skewer is inserted. Always preheat the oven, grill, or broiler and rack.

To poach boneless breasts: Marinate if desired. Oil or butter a shallow pan. Place breasts in pan in a single layer and add seasoning as desired, along with marinade, stock, or wine almost to cover. Cover the pan, heat on stove top or in 325°F oven and simmer for 20 minutes.

To bake boneless breasts: Marinate if desired. Brush with butter or oil, and place in one layer in a shallow pan. Season as desired. Cover pan and bake in a 425°F oven for 20 minutes.

To sauté boneless breasts: Heat butter or oil (or a combination) in a heavy skillet or sauté pan over moderate heat. Pound the breasts to flatten, then dredge in flour or other seasoning as desired. Place in the pan (do not crowd) and sauté for 8 to 12 minutes depending upon size; keep the pan moving over the flame and turn the meat from time to time. If you must sauté in batches, place the cooked breasts in a *warm* oven and cover loosely.

To broil or grill boneless breasts: Pound the breasts to flatten; marinate if desired. Brush the grill or broiler rack with butter or oil, and arrange the breasts on top. Brush the breasts with butter or oil and broil 5 to 6 inches from the heat for 4 to 5 minutes on a side; brush with butter or oil after turning.

To cook cutlets (horizontally sliced breast halves): Brush with butter or oil and seasoning if desired; grill, broil, or sauté for 2 to 3 minutes per side.

As there is not always a distinction in the market between boneless breasts, boneless breast halves, and cutlets or filets, recipes in this book always call for whole or half breasts, and indicate how to cut them. This is not so that you must skin, bone, or filet them yourself, but so that you can correctly judge the quantity to buy—usually one-third to one-half pound boneless chicken per person, depending upon appetite and other ingredients in the recipe.

There is really nothing easier to prepare than a succulent, nourishing, and delicious roast chicken.

CUT-UP CHICKENS

Cut-up chicken can be prepared in many ways. In most recipes, you can use whatever parts suit you. If the ingredients list calls for one cut-up or quartered chicken, you can certainly use all thighs or all breasts, as you wish. Cooking time will vary with the size of the bird, the size of the pieces, and the individual oven or grill; the meat is done if the juices run clear when a skewer is inserted into the flesh. Here are some guidelines on cooking times: White meat cooks faster than dark; you can add the breasts and wings to the cooking pan 10 to 15 minutes after starting the thighs and drumsticks, or remove them and keep warm if they are done early. One hour is usually sufficient for cooking a cut-up broiler/fryer, whether on the grill, in the oven, or on the stove top. Allow 1¼ to 1½ hours to cook a chicken that is quartered. If your recipe calls for cooking the chicken *uncovered*, check it from time to time and baste it to keep it from drying out; do this even if there is sauce in the pan.

RECIPES

Avocado and Chicken on Pumpernickel

This is an appealing open-face sandwich that can be cut in half or quarters to serve as an appetizer. Double or increase the recipe as necessary.

1	large avocado, peeled and seeded
	Juice of 1 lemon
¼	cup bright green snow peas or bean sprouts
4	to **5** slices pumpernickel bread
	Fresh mint sprigs for garnish

For the salad:

1½	cups cooked chicken, chopped
2	shallots, finely chopped
4	teaspoons pine nuts
1½	teaspoons chopped fresh mint
2½	to **3** tablespoons mayonnaise, or to taste

Cut the avocado into thin slices and sprinkle with the lemon juice.

Combine the salad ingredients in a bowl and mix well. Divide the sprouts on the bread, top with the salad, followed by the avocado slices. Garnish with mint sprigs.

Makes 1½ cups salad, enough to top 4 to 5 slices of bread.

Almond-Crisped Chicken Bits with Spiced Ginger Sauce

The chicken can be served hot or cold, so you can prepare the sauce or the entire recipe ahead of time if you wish.

For the sauce:

4	teaspoons grated fresh ginger
1	teaspoon whole allspice
1	teaspoon whole peppercorns
½	teaspoon mustard seed
½	teaspoon whole cloves
⅔	cup dry white wine
¼	cup white vinegar
2	to **3** tablespoons soy sauce

For the chicken:

1	cup bread crumbs (unseasoned)
1	cup ground almonds
	Salt and freshly ground pepper, if desired
1	egg
¼	cup milk
⅓	cup flour
6	chicken breast halves, bone and skin removed, cut into bite-size pieces
	Oil for frying

To make the sauce, combine the ginger and spices in a mortar and crush lightly. (If you do not have a mortar, place them between sheets of wax paper and crush with a rolling pin.) Combine with the wine and vinegar and soy sauce in a small saucepan. Bring slowly to a boil, and simmer for 8 minutes. Strain into a shallow serving bowl suitable for dipping.

Combine the bread crumbs and almonds in a shallow bowl or pie pan. Beat the egg and milk together in a small bowl. Put the flour in another shallow bowl. Roll the chicken in the flour, dip in the egg, and then roll in the almond-bread crumb mix. Place on wax paper till ready to cook. Heat a few tablespoons of oil in a skillet (the amount will depend on size of pan, but use as little as possible) and stir-fry chicken (in batches) till brown on all sides; drain on paper towels. Serve with the sauce on the side for dipping.

Serves 12 as an appetizer.

Avocado and Chicken on Pumpernickel makes wonderful picnic fare.

Easy Chicken Liver Pâté

Here is a simple, elegant, and inexpensive pâté. Make it in small ramekins for hostess or holiday gifts.

1 *pound chicken livers*
4 *tablespoons dry sherry*
½ *cup butter*
2 *shallots, finely chopped*
1 *clove garlic, crushed*
¼ *cup heavy cream*
1 *teaspoon fresh or ¼ teaspoon dried thyme leaves*
¼ *teaspoon ground allspice*
      Salt and freshly ground pepper to taste

Place the livers in a bowl. Pour the sherry over them and let stand for 2 hours. Drain and reserve the liquid.

Melt 2 tablespoons of the butter in a skillet over medium heat. Add the livers, shallots, and garlic, and cook, stirring occasionally, for 3 minutes or until livers lose their pink color. Pour in the reserved liquid and cook for 1 minute. Remove the pan from the heat.

Melt the remaining butter in another pan and measure 2 tablespoons of it into the container of a food processor or blender. Add the livers, cream, thyme, and allspice and puree until smooth. Season with salt and pepper. Spoon into a terrine or ramekins and pour the remaining melted butter over the top. Store covered in the refrigerator, but bring to room temperature before serving.

Serve with French bread, cornichons, and spicy mustard.

Makes 3 to 4 cups pâté.

Country Chicken Soup

This hearty soup will revive anyone suffering from winter's chill.

3 *quarts chicken stock*
4 *chicken breast halves, bone and skin removed*
1 *teaspoon whole black peppercorns*
4 *bay leaves*
1 *sprig fresh rosemary*
1 *onion, peeled and chopped*
1 *red pepper, cored, seeded, and chopped*
2 *carrots, chopped*
½ *pound cabbage, shredded*
6 *ounces macaroni or other small pasta shapes*
2 *tablespoons Parmesan cheese, additional to pass if desired*

Bring the stock to a boil in a large saucepan. Add the chicken breasts, peppercorns, bay leaves, and rosemary. Reduce the heat, cover, and simmer for 20 minutes or until chicken is tender.

Remove chicken from pan and set aside. Strain the liquid and return to a clean saucepan. Stir in the onion, red pepper, carrots, cabbage, and pasta. Cover, bring to a simmer, and cook gently for 10 minutes, or until pasta is almost cooked.

Meanwhile, slice the chicken, then stir it into the soup and cook for about 5 minutes, until pasta is done and chicken is hot. Just before serving, stir the Parmesan through the soup.

Makes about 5 quarts.

Chicken, Leek, and Chick-Pea Soup

This subtly flavored soup takes on a little punch if coriander is substituted for the parsley and a pinch of chili powder is added to the leeks.

1 *quart chicken stock*
½ *cup tiny pasta shapes*
2 *tablespoons butter*
1 *leek, white part only, cleaned and thinly sliced*
1 *clove garlic, peeled and sliced*
½ *cup cooked and lightly roasted chick-peas*
4 *teaspoons flour*
3 *tablespoons chopped parsley*
      Pinch of cayenne pepper
      Salt and freshly ground pepper
1 *cup chopped cooked chicken*

Bring the chicken stock to a boil in a saucepan and cook the pasta in it until just done. Remove the pasta with a slotted spoon and keep the stock at a simmer.

Meanwhile, melt the butter in a heavy saucepan over medium heat and sauté the leek and garlic until just golden, about 5 minutes. Add the chick-peas, toss for a minute, sprinkle with flour, and sauté for 10 to 15 seconds. Add the hot stock gradually, stirring constantly. Add the parsley, cayenne, and salt and pepper as desired. Add the pasta and chicken, return to a boil, and serve.

Makes about 2 quarts.

Quick and Simple Chicken Vegetable Soup

This is a very simple way to pull a nourishing soup together. If you like, you can reserve the chicken to use in any recipe calling for cooked chicken, and eat the vegetable soup on its own. Use chicken breasts with the bone still in to give a good flavor.

4   *chicken breast halves, skin removed*
8   *cups water*
4   *medium onions, peeled, or leeks, trimmed and cleaned*
2   *cups chopped celery*
4   *to **6** large carrots, sliced crosswise*
2   *cups fresh or frozen green peas*
2   *tablespoons herbes de Provence*
       Salt and freshly ground pepper to taste

Place the chicken breasts, water, and onions or leeks in a large saucepan and bring to a boil. Reduce the heat and simmer for 30 minutes, skimming off any fat as it rises.

Add the celery and carrots and simmer 15 minutes. Remove the chicken breasts and pull the meat from the bone, shredding it into bite-size pieces (it should fall easily from the bone). Season the soup with the herbes de Provence and the salt and pepper. Add the chicken with the peas to the soup and cook until hot. Serve immediately, accompanied by crusty bread.

Makes about 4 quarts.

When you are in the mood for a light but warming meal, try Quick and Simple Chicken Vegetable Soup. Serve it with fresh, crusty bread and perhaps a bit of cheese.

Curried Chicken Soup

Here is a delightfully thick and spicy soup.

1	*tablespoon olive oil*
1	*tablespoon butter*
½	*cup chopped celery*
½	*cup chopped zucchini*
½	*cup chopped onion*
1	*tablespoon flour*
2	*teaspoons curry powder*
1	*quart chicken stock*
1	*chicken breast half, skin and bone removed, and cut into julienne strips*
½	*cup cooked rice*
1	*Granny Smith apple, cored and diced*
1	*tablespoon chopped fresh coriander leaves*
	Salt and freshly ground pepper to taste

Heat the oil and butter in a heavy saucepan over medium heat, add the celery, zucchini, and onion, and sauté until tender, about 10 minutes. Stir in the flour and curry powder and cook for 3 to 4 minutes. Stir in the chicken stock, blend well, raise the heat, and bring to a boil. Add the chicken, reduce the heat, and simmer for 15 minutes. Add the rice and the apple, and simmer 20 minutes more. Stir in the coriander and season to taste with salt and pepper. Serve immediately.

Makes about 2 quarts.

There is no reason to confine chicken soup to the sickroom. Spicy Curried Chicken Soup, made with apple and zucchini, is an exotic variant for the hearty diner.

A WORD ON MARINADES

Marinades are acidic sauces in which foods are soaked before they are cooked. The purpose of a marinade is to enhance the flavor of the dish to be prepared by infusing it with a complementary seasoning. Marinades also have a tenderizing effect that increases with the length of the soaking period. However, since birds should not be held for more than a few days before cooking, it is wise to rely on a moist cooking method to tenderize one that is old. Marinades are sometimes cooked to blend their flavors. These should be cooled before they are applied to the raw food. Because marinades are acidic and will react with aluminum, they should always be used in stainless, glass, ceramic, or plastic containers, and the food should be turned with stainless, wooden, or plastic utensils. If you do not have a bowl or pan of the right size, you can let poultry (or anything else) marinate in a resealable plastic bag. This may also save space in the refrigerator.

The longer food sits in a marinade, the more flavor it will absorb; and foods marinated at room temperature absorb flavor more quickly than they do chilled. Poultry and game birds are usually marinated in the refrigerator for anywhere from eight hours to two days; if you fail to plan ahead, you can have reasonable seasoning success marinating them for two hours at room temperature. Strongly flavored marinades can overpower the natural flavor of the flesh if left on for too long, so bear that in mind when you experiment with recipes—especially with game birds, which have lovely flavors of their own. Unless you eat pheasant, partridge, or quail as a matter of course, you will want to really taste it, so use a light hand with any marinades for birds with which you are not particularly familiar.

There are many marinade recipes in this book; they can be used fairly interchangeably on the different birds as long as you consider the cooking and flavor characteristics of whatever you are preparing. Marinades are not difficult to invent if you enjoy experimenting, so adapt as suits your mood—or the ingredients at hand. Most marinades have either wine, lemon juice, or vinegar as a base and are seasoned with herbs and/or spices. They often contain cooking oil as well. Marinades are sometimes reserved and used in a sauce for the completed dish, so don't toss them without reading a recipe all the way through. Do not, however, serve the liquid in which the food has been marinating without cooking it, since it may contain bacteria. You may mix a marinade before you plan to use it, but do not reuse; discard if it is not a component of the sauce.

Chicken Salad South of the Border

This is a zesty salad in a pretty serving.

For the marinade:
½   cup freshly squeezed lime juice
¼   cup olive oil
1   heaping tablespoon chili mustard, or
    1 teaspoon Dijon mustard mixed with
    1 teaspoon hot chili paste
1   teaspoon honey
1   teaspoon salt
2   large jalapeño peppers, seeded and
    chopped

For the salad:
6   chicken breast halves, bone and skin
    removed
1   quart safflower oil, for frying
6   to 8 fresh corn flour tortillas
¼   cup chopped fresh coriander leaves
½   cup red wine vinegar
1   large tomato, coarsely chopped
1   large head romaine lettuce, shredded
2   small avocados, cut into thirds, then
    thinly sliced
2   limes cut into thin wedges

Combine the ingredients for the marinade in a large bowl and mix until well blended. Add the chicken breasts and toss to coat well. Let sit at room temperature for 1 hour.

Meanwhile, cook the tortillas one at a time. Heat the safflower oil to 350°F in a heavy 4-quart saucepan. Use a double fry-basket or two ladles as follows: Place a tortilla in the larger basket or ladle, then gently press the other basket or ladle into it to make it take the basket shape; immerse in the hot oil. As soon as the tortilla holds the shape, remove the baskets. Baste the tortilla with hot oil to cook through and fry for 2 to 3

minutes, until golden brown. Remove from oil and drain on paper towels.

Brush the hot grill with a little oil and cook chicken breasts for 7 to 10 minutes on a side, or until golden and cooked through. Remove from grill and let sit about 10 minutes, then tear into thin strips and place in a medium-size bowl with the vinegar and coriander. Toss to mix well.

To serve, spread a handful of lettuce over each plate and sprinkle with about 1 tablespoon of chopped tomato. Place a tortilla in the center; fill with a cup of chicken salad. Garnish each plate with a fan of avocado slices and the lime wedges.

Serves 4 to 6.

Thai Chicken with Coriander Peanut Dressing

This is a warm salad. Serve it for a winter luncheon or light supper.

6½ ounces cellophane noodles
1½ cups cooked, shredded chicken
1   cup grated carrots
¼   cup chopped fresh coriander leaves
1   medium cucumber, chopped
2   cloves garlic, peeled and crushed
¼   cup soy sauce
¼   cup freshly squeezed lime juice
4   tablespoons peanut butter
5   tablespoons mild-flavored
    vegetable oil
1   tablespoon brown sugar
¼   cup shelled peanuts, chopped

Place the noodles in a large heatproof bowl and pour boiling water over them. Let stand for 10 minutes, then drain. Combine the chicken, carrots, coriander, and cucumber in another bowl. Combine the garlic, soy sauce, lime juice, peanut butter, oil, and sugar in a saucepan; bring to a boil and simmer for 3 minutes. Pour over the chicken mixture and toss to mix well.

Serve immediately, making a bed of noodles topped with chicken on each plate and sprinkling peanuts over all.

Serves 4.

Festive Chicken Salad South of the Border is great for warm-weather entertaining.

Smoked Chicken and New Potato Salad

The flavor of smoked chicken is not dissimilar to that of ham and works well with tender new potatoes, apple, chives, and parsley. You can prepare this a day ahead if you like; the flavor will improve as it sits, but don't add the radicchio until ready to serve. Serve chilled or at room temperature.

For the salad:

8	*new potatoes*
3	*tablespoons fresh chopped chives*
¼	*cup fresh chopped parsley*
½	*cup shredded radicchio*
1	*crisp, tart apple, preferably red*
1	*pound boneless smoked chicken breast*
	Freshly ground pepper to taste
8	*asparagus spears*
	Fresh greens, washed and dried

For the dressing:

1	*teaspoon Dijon mustard*
2	*tablespoons white or thyme vinegar*
4	*tablespoons olive oil*

Wash the new potatoes and boil until crisply tender, about 20 minutes. Drain and rinse under cold water. While they cool, mix the dressing: In a small bowl or jar, whisk the mustard into the vinegar to dissolve, then whisk in the oil. As soon as the potatoes are cool enough to handle, cut them into ⅛-inch slices and put in a large bowl. Add the chives and parsley and toss with about half the dressing. When the potatoes are completely cool, add the radicchio. Core the apple, cut into very small pieces, and add to the potatoes. Remove the skin from the chicken if desired, cut or tear into bite-size pieces, and add to the potatoes. Toss to mix well, season with pepper, and set aside.

Blanch the asparagus spears by steaming or boiling for 3 to 4 minutes until bright green and just tender. Plunge in cold water and let cool. Before serving, taste the salad; add more dressing if desired. Arrange the greens and asparagus in a ring on a serving platter and drizzle with the remaining dressing, then place the chicken and potato salad in the center.

Serves 3 to 4.

Smoked Chicken and New Potato Salad.

Grilled Orange Chicken with Salad

The orange gives this chicken a wonderful fresh taste. Reserve part of the marinade to dress the salad.

For the marinade:
½ cup freshly squeezed orange juice
¼ cup champagne vinegar
    Grated rind of 1 navel orange
½ cup olive oil
    Salt and freshly ground pepper to taste

4 chicken breast halves, bone and skin removed, cut into 2-inch strips

For the salad:
1 bunch watercress
1 small head red lettuce
3 small mandarin oranges, peeled, sectioned, and seeded, or 1 8-ounce can mandarin orange sections, drained

Mix the marinade ingredients in a small bowl. Place the chicken strips in another bowl and pour all but 3 tablespoons of the marinade over them, turning to coat. Cover and refrigerate for at least 3 hours.

Wash and dry the salad greens. Trim the watercress and tear the lettuce into small pieces. Toss together in a bowl and keep cool until ready to use.

Brush the hot grill with oil and cook the chicken strips for 2 to 3 minutes on each side, then cool to room temperature. Toss the reserved marinade in with the greens and divide them onto plates. Divide chicken strips and place over salad, season with more fresh pepper if desired, and garnish with mandarin orange sections.

Serves 4.

Chicken Salad with Thyme and Spanish Onions

Spanish onions give a fresh and colorful punch to this thyme-infused salad.

6 chicken breast halves, bone and skin removed
5 tablespoons oil
3 tablespoons red wine vinegar
4 teaspoons fresh thyme leaves
    Salt and freshly ground pepper
1 head Bibb lettuce, washed and dried
½ bunch escarole, washed and dried
2 Spanish onions, sliced paper thin and separated into rings

Pound the chicken breast to thin somewhat and cut into 1-inch-wide strips. Heat 2 tablespoons of the oil in a skillet and stir-fry the chicken in batches until just cooked, adding a little more oil if necessary. Remove from the pan and add the vinegar, stir to mix with the juices, and strain into a small bowl or jar. Add the thyme and about 2½ tablespoons of oil and blend well. Season with salt and pepper as desired.

Arrange the Bibb lettuce and the escarole on a serving plate. Top with the chicken and onion rings. Pour the thyme dressing over all just before serving.

Serves 4 to 6.

Tarragon Chicken Salad

This is a lovely hot-weather salad. If possible, use grilled chicken.

For the salad:
1 cup broken walnut pieces
4 cups cooked chicken, skinned, boned, and cut in bite-size pieces
2 cups seedless green grapes, halved if desired
½ cup finely sliced endive
    Fresh greens, washed and dried

For the dressing:
2 teaspoons Dijon mustard
2 tablespoons white or tarragon vinegar
3 tablespoons fresh tarragon leaves, coarsely chopped
1 tablespoon fresh chives, minced
6 tablespoons oil, preferably a combination of walnut and olive
    Salt and freshly ground pepper to taste

Toast the walnuts in a shallow pan in a 350°F oven for about 15 minutes or until lightly browned. Combine all of the salad ingredients except the fresh greens in a large bowl. In a small bowl or jar, whisk the mustard into the vinegar to dissolve and add the tarragon and chives. Whisk in the oil. Toss only as much dressing as necessary in with the chicken mixture and season with salt and pepper if desired. Chill for at least one hour. Serve on a bed of fresh greens.

Serves 4 to 6.

Grilled Orange Chicken served on a bed of greens is the perfect meal on a hot summer day.

Grilled Chicken with Oregano

Oregano and lemon combine to give this grill a Mediterranean aroma. A wonderful variation for supremes follows.

For the marinade:
Grated rind and juice of 2 lemons
½ cup olive oil
Freshly ground pepper to taste
4 tablespoons chopped fresh oregano

1 cut-up broiler/fryer
Salt, if desired

Whisk the marinade ingredients together in small bowl. Season the chicken pieces with salt if desired, and place in a shallow dish. Pour the marinade over them and turn to coat both sides. Cover and refrigerate at least 8 hours.

Brush the hot grill with oil, and cook the chicken on it, covered, for 25 to 30 minutes on each side, or until done.

Serves 3 to 4.

Grilled Oregano Supremes with Fresh Tomato and Feta Topping

This variation on the previous recipe brings the Mediterranean even closer. Save this for tomato season.

Lemon-oregano marinade (see previous recipe)
6 chicken breast halves, bone and skin removed
3 ripe tomatoes, diced
½ cup crumbled feta cheese
1 tablespoon fresh oregano
Freshly ground pepper

Pound the chicken breasts to flatten slightly, place in a bowl, and pour the marinade over them, turning to coat. Cover and refrigerate for at least 8 hours.

Mix the tomatoes, feta, and oregano in a small bowl, and season with pepper. Brush the hot grill with oil, and cook the chicken, covered, for 5 to 7 minutes on one side. Turn the chicken, spoon the tomato mix over it, and cook until done, another 5 to 7 minutes.

Serves 4 to 6.

Classic Fried Chicken with Herbs

Make this for a picnic or party—it's great hot or cold. If you double the recipe, don't double the oil; just add more to the pan as needed. Use a frying thermometer for accuracy.

5 cups vegetable oil
2 large eggs
⅔ cup buttermilk
⅓ cup lemon juice
1 teaspoon salt, or as desired
1¼ teaspoons freshly ground pepper
1 tablespoon fresh or 2 teaspoons dried thyme
1 tablespoon fresh or 2 teaspoons dried oregano
2 cups seasoned dry bread crumbs small broiler/fryers, each cut into 8 pieces

In a 12-inch skillet or electric frying pan over medium-high heat, heat 4 cups of oil to 375°F, or until a 1-inch cube of white bread turns brown in it in 60 seconds.

While the oil heats, combine the eggs, buttermilk, lemon juice, salt and pepper, and herbs in a medium-size bowl; beat with a whisk until well blended. Place the bread crumbs in another bowl or pie pan. One piece at a time, dip the chicken in the egg mixture, lift, and let excess drip back into bowl, then dredge on all sides in the bread crumbs. Place the chicken in the hot oil, adding only as many pieces as will fit in one layer without crowding. Cover and cook for 5 to 6 minutes on a side, or until cooked through; use tongs to turn. Transfer cooked chicken to a platter or cookie sheet lined with wax paper; if planning to serve hot, keep in the oven set on warm. Add more oil to the pan if necessary and reheat it to 375°F before adding more chicken. Fry the remaining chicken.

Serves 6.

Chicken Yakitori

This wonderful classic can be served as an appetizer or main course. Either way do not overcook and serve very hot. Double the recipe as needed.

Note: You can, of course, use this same marinade for half or quartered chickens or split Cornish game hens.

1	large clove garlic, peeled and minced
2	inches fresh ginger, peeled and minced
¼	cup mirin wine
½	cup white wine vinegar
1	tablespoon soy sauce
1	tablespoon sesame oil
½	cup vegetable oil
2	tablespoons dry sherry
4	chicken breast halves, bone and skin removed, cut into 1-inch cubes

Mix all ingredients except the chicken in a large bowl; blend well. Add the chicken and toss to coat. Cover and refrigerate for 3 hours.

Place the chicken on skewers; if desired, divide so that each diner can be served an individual skewer. Brush the hot grill with oil and cook chicken 7 to 10 minutes, turning frequently, until golden brown. Serve immediately.

Serves 4 as a main course, 6 as an appetizer.

Tarragon-Mustard Grilled Chicken or Cornish Game Hen

This delicious recipe belies the simplicity of its preparation. Try this marinade on turkey burgers as well.

For the marinade:

1	tablespoon white or tarragon vinegar
3	tablespoons Dijon mustard
1	tablespoon olive oil
1	clove garlic, peeled and crushed
3	tablespoons minced tarragon leaves
1	broiler/fryer, cut as desired, or 2 Cornish game hens, split or halved Salt and freshly ground pepper to taste

In a small bowl, mix the vinegar and mustard well with a fork, then blend in the oil. Stir in the garlic and tarragon. Season the chicken with the salt and pepper, if desired, then spread the marinade on all sides of each piece. Place in a bowl, cover, and refrigerate for at least 8 hours.

Brush the hot grill with oil, and cook the chicken, covered, for one hour or until done, turning once.

Serves 3 to 4.

Stir-Fry Chicken with Cashews

A variation on an Oriental classic. Be sure to have all the ingredients cut up before you begin to cook so that it can go together quickly. Serve over rice.

4	chicken breast halves, bone and skin removed
1	head of broccoli, florets only
2	tablespoons olive oil, more if needed
1	red onion, peeled and cut into petals
1	carrot, sliced diagonally
1	clove garlic, peeled and crushed
½	inch fresh ginger, peeled and grated
3	tablespoons unsalted cashews
½	cup stock
2	teaspoons cornstarch
2	teaspoons soy sauce
1	tablespoon sherry
¼	teaspoon sesame oil
3	scallions, sliced diagonally

Cut each chicken breast horizontally into 2 filets, then into strips about 1×3 inches. Steam the broccoli for 5 minutes, or until tender and bright green, then plunge in cold water.

Heat the oil in a skillet over medium heat and sauté the carrot and onion for 5 minutes. Add the garlic and ginger, cook 1 minute. Remove from the pan. Raise the heat a little and sauté chicken, in batches, until just lightly browned; remove from the pan. Lower the heat to medium and sauté the broccoli and cashews until the nuts are lightly browned.

Whisk the stock, cornstarch, soy sauce, sherry, and sesame oil together. Return the vegetables and chicken to the pan with the scallions, raise the heat a little, pour in the liquid, and cook until it boils and thickens. Serve immediately.

Serves 4.

Chicken with Parsleyed Green Beans

This is a very quick dish. Be sure to start with fresh beans—use slender *haricots verts* if possible.

4 *chicken breast halves, skin and bone removed*
2 *tablespoons pine nuts*
1½ *pounds green beans, tips trimmed*
2 *tablespoons olive oil, more if needed*
4 *cloves garlic, peeled and minced, or to taste*
4 *tablespoons chopped fresh parsley*
1 *tablespoon butter*
Juice of ½ lemon
Salt and freshly ground pepper to taste

Cut each chicken breast horizontally into 2 filets, then into strips about 1 × 3 inches. Put the pine nuts in a small pan and toast in a 350°F oven for 5 to 7 minutes, or until golden. Steam the beans for 3 to 5 minutes, or until tender and bright green, then plunge in cold water.

Heat the oil in a skillet over medium-high heat and sauté the chicken, in batches if necessary, until just barely cooked. Remove from pan. Lower the heat, add the garlic and parsley, and cook for 1 minute. Add the beans and chicken and cook, stirring until hot. Add the lemon juice while stirring, then the butter and pine nuts. Season with salt and pepper and serve at once.

Serves 4.

Chicken Supremes with Sesame

Sesame seeds and chicken are lovely together. Indulge yourself and use enough butter to turn these golden without sticking to the pan.

6 *chicken breast halves, skin and bone removed*
Salt and freshly ground pepper to taste
¾ *cup sesame seeds, on a plate*
6 *tablespoons unsalted butter*
Juice of 1 lemon

Pound chicken breasts lightly to flatten somewhat and season with salt and pepper if desired. Dredge on both sides in sesame seeds.

Heat half the butter over high heat in a skillet just large enough to hold all the chicken, add the chicken, and cook for 5 minutes on each side. Transfer to a serving dish and keep warm. Heat the remaining butter in the skillet, add the lemon juice, swirl until the mix turns nutty brown. Pour over the chicken and serve at once.

Serves 6.

Chicken with Parsleyed Green Beans, served here on a bed of rice.

Supremes with Almonds and Herbs

Here is a variation on the classic chicken Kiev—boneless chicken breasts stuffed with butter and chives. Almonds and mustard have been added for an interesting combination of flavors. Use a frying thermometer for accuracy.

For the filling:
6 *tablespoons butter*
2 *teaspoons Dijon mustard*
⅓ *cup chopped almonds*
1 *tablespoon chopped fresh parsley*
4 *teaspoons fresh chopped chives*
   Freshly ground pepper

For the chicken:
4 *chicken breast halves, bone and skin removed*
½ *cup flour*
   Freshly ground pepper
2 *eggs*
⅓ *cup milk*
1½ *cups fresh white bread crumbs*
   Oil for frying

Blend the ingredients for the filling with a fork; divide and shape into four 4-inch-long logs. Place on wax paper and chill until firm.

Pound the chicken breasts to make quite thin; do not tear the flesh. Place a roll of butter in the center of each and fold the ends of the filet over it, then roll up to enclose. If the flesh does not stick to itself, secure with toothpicks.

Place the flour in a shallow bowl and season with pepper. In another bowl, beat the egg lightly with the milk. Place the bread crumbs on a plate. Dip each piece of rolled-up chicken in the flour, then in the egg mix, and then roll in the bread crumbs to coat. Place on a plate covered with wax paper, cover with wax paper, and refrigerate for 1 hour so the crumbs are well adhered.

Fill a deep skillet or electric frying pan with enough oil to cover the chicken rolls. Heat to 375°F or until a 1-inch cube of white bread turns brown in it in 60 seconds. Add the chicken and cook until golden brown on all sides, 5 to 8 minutes. Drain on paper towels and serve.

Serves 4.

Baked Chicken with Sage and Salt Dough Crust

Here seasoned chickens are completely encased in flour, salt, and water that dries during baking to form a hard crust, trapping all the juices and suffusing the birds with the flavor of sage and garlic. The crust is discarded once the birds are done, so don't be alarmed by the amount of salt.

2 *large whole broiler/fryers, 3½ to 4 pounds each*
2 *to **4** bunches fresh sage leaves, plus extra for garnish*
   Ground white pepper
30 *cloves garlic*
4 *cups flour*
4 *cups kosher salt*

Refer to *How to Roast a Whole Chicken*, page 15. Beginning at the neck cavity, carefully loosen the skin over the birds' breasts and slide 3 or 4 leaves of sage onto the flesh. Season the remaining sage with white pepper, divide, and place half in the cavity of each bird along with 15 cloves of garlic. Truss the birds.

Combine the flour and salt in a large mixing bowl and add enough cold water to make a spreadable paste. Divide between the birds and spread so as to completely encase each in dough; no part of the chickens should show.

Place in a roasting pan in a 425°F oven and bake for 45 minutes or until the dough is golden brown. Remove from the oven and let rest for 10 minutes. Remove the crust—use a sharp knife if necessary—and discard. Arrange a bed of sage leaves on a serving platter and top with the chickens; carve or cut them at the table.

Serves 4 to 6.

Cornish Game Hen with Orange-Fennel Cognac Sauce

The slightly sweet sauce for this dish can be prepared a day or two ahead of time and refrigerated, because the flavor improves as it ages. You can, of course, prepare whole chickens (or try pheasant) in the same way.

For the hens:
4 *small Cornish game hens*
2 *lemons, halved*
   Bunch of fennel leaves
   Salt and freshly ground pepper to taste

For the sauce:

2	tablespoons olive oil
1	cup chopped fennel bulb
2	large shallots, peeled and chopped
1	tablespoon fresh thyme leaves
6	juniper berries
2	oranges
⅓	cup cognac

Refer to *How to Roast a Whole Chicken*, page 15. Squeeze the lemons over the hens, sprinkle with some of the fennel leaves, cover, and marinate in the refrigerator for 6 to 8 hours or at room temperature for two hours; reserve the lemon peels.

Prepare the sauce while the bird is marinating. Heat the olive oil in a small saucepan and cook the fennel, shallots, and thyme in it briefly. Add the juniper berries. Squeeze and strain the juice from the oranges into the fennel, add the orange peel, and simmer, covered, for 10 minutes. Remove the orange peel and stir in the cognac. Simmer to reduce somewhat. Serve warm or at room temperature.

Preheat the oven to 450°F. Season the hens with salt and pepper, place some lemon peel and fennel leaves into their cavities, and truss them. Place them on a rack in a shallow roasting pan. Spoon some of the sauce over the hens and place them in the oven. Lower the temperature to 350°F and roast until done, about 40 minutes, basting with drippings and more of the sauce from time to time.

Serves 4.

People often complain that they cannot make decent gravy, but there is really no mystery to this essential finish to many a roasted bird. The most important thing is to eliminate all but a few tablespoons of grease from the pan juices, and to completely dissolve the flour in the remaining grease before adding the hot broth. Here are two versions.

While the bird is roasting, place the neck and giblets in a medium-size saucepan with a whole onion, celery rib with leaves, carrot, and any other vegetables desired for flavor—leeks, garlic, or shallots are wonderful additions. Add a bay leaf, fresh or dried thyme, and a few peppercorns, and cover with cold water. (If you want to make a lot of gravy, buy additional giblets and necks and increase the amount of the other ingredients appropriately.) Bring to a boil, cover, reduce the heat, and simmer for 15 minutes. Remove the liver and continue to simmer the rest on the lowest possible heat until the neck is done, from about 30 minutes for chicken to as much as an hour for turkey. If the liquid evaporates, add more water. When the neck is done, remove the broth from the heat, strain it, and reserve for the gravy. There should be about 2 cups; if not, add water. If desired, chop the giblets and reserve them as well.

When the bird comes out of the oven, transfer it to a platter to rest and skim as much grease as possible from the roasting pan; transfer 3 tablespoons of the grease to a small saucepan. Add the reserved broth to the roasting pan, heat it, and stir to blend in the drippings. Stir 3 tablespoons of flour into the saucepan with the grease; dissolve the flour completely, then heat the mixture and cook over a medium heat for about five minutes, stirring constantly. Add the broth with the pan drippings to the flour mixture and simmer until thick, stirring frequently. Stir in the chopped giblets just before serving and heat through.

For a richer finish to your gravy, blend equal parts of butter and flour with your fingers and shape them into small balls. Skim as much of the grease as possible from the roasting pan. Add the reserved broth to the roasting pan, heat it, and stir to blend in the drippings. Drop the flour-and-butter balls into the hot broth and stir until dissolved and the broth is thickened—allow 2 to 4 tablespoons of this mixture for every cup of broth. Stir in the chopped giblets just before serving and heat through.

Honey and Grain-Mustard Chicken or Cornish Hens

Mustard is a wonderful complement for poultry. Here it is combined with honey in an unusual marinade.

For the marinade:

1	tablespoon grainy mustard
1	tablespoon cider vinegar
1	tablespoon honey
1	small shallot, minced
1	tablespoon dry white wine
¼	cup vegetable oil
1	teaspoon fresh or ¼ teaspoon dried thyme
	Salt and freshly ground pepper to taste
2	broiler/fryers or **4** Cornish game hens, halved

Combine the marinade ingredients in a small bowl and blend well. Place the birds in a roasting pan large enough to hold them in one layer (or use two pans) and coat with the marinade on all sides. Cover and refrigerate for at least 8 hours, turning occasionally.

Bake in the marinade in a 350°F oven until done (about 35 to 40 minutes for Cornish hens, 60 minutes for chickens).

Serves 4 to 6.

Cornish Hen baked in Honey and Grain-Mustard marinade. You can cook this dish on a grill if you like.

Roast Pistachio Chicken or Capon with Citrus Sauce

Sometimes we forget that a simple roast chicken is delicious. Here is a version stuffed with fragrant basmati rice and pistachios, served with warm citrus sauce.

Note: If you use a capon, double the recipes for the stuffing and sauce.

For the stuffing:

2	cups cooked basmati rice
½	cup shelled and chopped pistachios
1	tablespoon drained green peppercorns
1	onion, peeled and grated
1	small carrot, grated
¼	teaspoon ground cardamom
1	roasting chicken, 5 to 6 pounds

For the sauce:

1	orange, plus additional orange juice to total 1 cup
2	tablespoons orange marmalade
1	tablespoon red currant jelly
2	teaspoons Dijon mustard

Refer to *How To Roast a Whole Chicken*, page 15. Mix the ingredients for the stuffing together in a bowl. Stuff and truss the bird, place in a 450°F oven, lower the heat to 350°F, and roast 25 minutes per pound for chicken, 20 minutes per pound for capon.

Note: Refer to *How to Stuff and Truss a Bird*, page 106, and *How to Roast a Whole Bird*, page 108.

Prepare the sauce while the bird is roasting. Peel the orange with a vegetable peeler and finely chop the peel. Then drop it into a small pan of boiling water, simmer for 2 minutes, and drain. Squeeze the orange and supplement with orange juice to make 1 cup. Combine orange juice with remaining ingredients in a small saucepan, stir and bring to a boil, reduce heat, and simmer until the sauce is reduced by half. Strain, if desired, and add the chopped orange peel. Spoon the hot sauce over each portion of the roast bird.

The chicken serves 6 to 7, the capon 8 to 10.

Simple Curried Chicken

This recipe is extremely easy to prepare. It is delicious hot or cold and makes wonderful chicken salad.

Note: Garam masala is a spice mixture found in Indian and specialty food markets. If not available, substitute 2 teaspoons curry powder.

½	*cup plain yogurt*
1	*tablespoon curry powder*
1	*teaspoon garam masala*
2	*to 3 onions, peeled and thinly sliced*
1	*broiler/fryer, cut up and skin removed*

Preheat the oven to 350°F. Mix the yogurt, curry powder, and garam masala. Cover the bottom of a shallow roasting pan with the onions. Spoon about one-third of the yogurt mixture over the onions. Put the chicken in the pan and top with the remainder of the yogurt mixture. Bake uncovered, basting occasionally, until done, 1 to 1½ hours, depending upon size.

Serves 3 to 4.

Simple Curried Chicken is perhaps the easiest imaginable curry recipe—and the onions are as tasty as the bird.

Basic Rice Stuffing

Rice makes wonderful poultry stuffing. It is as versatile as the birds in the ways that it can be seasoned—sweet, tart, or herbed; if you experiment with the many different types of rice, you will have a nearly endless variety of stuffings. Cook rice al dente for stuffings, otherwise it will be gluey when you take it out of the bird. If you like, sauté the rice in butter or oil before cooking it, and use stock or wine for some or all of the cooking liquid.

Note: Refer to *How to Stuff and Truss a Bird*, page 106, and *How to Roast a Whole Bird*, page 108.

3	*cups cooked converted or brown rice*
1	*carrot, diced*
1	*onion, peeled and diced*
2	*tablespoons butter, diced (optional)*
2	*to 3 tablespoons assorted chopped fresh herb leaves—rosemary, thyme, oregano, tarragon, fennel, dill, parsley*
	Salt and freshly ground pepper to taste

Mix all ingredients together and stuff the bird.

Makes about 4 cups stuffing, more than enough for one roasting chicken.

Note: Double the recipe as necessary, or add other ingredients as suggested below.

Variations:

• Substitute 1 cup wild rice for 1 cup of the converted or brown rice.

• Add ½ to 1 cup nuts—almonds, walnuts, pecans, pine; toast first in a shallow pan in a 350°F oven for 15 to 20 minutes, if desired (5 to 7 minutes for pine nuts).
• Add 1 tart or semi-tart apple, cored, peeled if desired, and chopped.
• Add 1 cup dried fruit—raisins, currants, apricots, pitted prunes; don't forget that they will swell during baking.
• Add browned chopped poultry livers, simmered with sherry or cognac if desired.
• Add a finely chopped lemon or orange, include the peel.
• Season with spices instead of herbs—nutmeg, cinnamon, cardamom, ginger, cloves (particularly nice with fruit).
• Add 6 to 12 chestnuts: To peel chestnuts easily, place them in a small saucepan and cover with water. Bring to a boil, then remove the pan from the heat. Using a slotted spoon, remove the nuts one at a time and, with a paring knife, peel off both the shell and the inner skin. Discard any flesh that is moldy; cut the chestnuts into small pieces.
• Use alliums other than onions—leeks, shallots, garlic—as appropriate to the bird and the menu.
• Add ½ to 1 cup mushrooms, using the familiar button type or some of the more exotic imported and dried varieties; sauté first if desired.

Chicken with Leeks and White Wine

A very easy and very tasty dish. Warn your guests to beware of the olive pits.

2 to **3** *leeks, white parts only, washed and thinly sliced*
4 *cloves garlic, peeled and finely chopped*
3 *tablespoons sun-dried tomatoes, coarsely chopped*
3 *tablespoons Niçoise olives*
1 *tablespoon herbes de Provence*
1 *cup dry white wine*
2 *tablespoons oil, preferably half olive and half walnut*
     Salt and freshly ground pepper to taste
1 *broiler/fryer, cut up and skin removed*

Preheat the oven to 350°F. Place all ingredients except chicken and ¼ cup of wine in a shallow roasting pan and mix well. Add the chicken and turn to coat with sauce. Bake uncovered, basting occasionally, until done, 1 to 1½ hours, depending upon size. Add the remaining wine about 10 minutes before the chicken is done.

Serves 3 to 4.

Chicken Normandy

Apples and onions make a simple semi-sweet sauce for baking chicken breasts. Be sure to remove the skin and all visible fat from the meat before cooking so that the sauce is not greasy.

6 *chicken breast halves, skin removed*
1 *tablespoon olive oil*
1 *onion, peeled and thinly sliced*
1½ *Granny Smith apples, cored and sliced*
2 *cups unsweetened apple juice*
2 to **3** *tablespoons honey*
2 *tablespoons calvados (optional)*
1 *tablespoon butter*
     Salt and freshly ground pepper to taste

Arrange the chicken breasts in one layer in a baking dish.

Heat the oil in a skillet over medium heat, and sauté the onions in it until golden, about 5 minutes. Add the apples and sauté 1 minute. Spoon the mixture over the chicken.

Combine the apple juice, honey, and calvados in a saucepan and bring to a boil. Remove from the heat and whisk in the butter. Season with salt and pepper if desired. Pour over the chicken. Bake in a 350°F oven until the chicken is done, about 45 minutes.

Serves 6.

Chicken with Tarragon

Tarragon, chicken, and white wine is a classic combination in French cuisine. This is an extremely easy way to prepare it.

4 *chicken breast halves, skin removed*
     Salt and freshly ground pepper to taste
2 *tablespoons chopped fresh tarragon*
     Juice of 1 lemon
1 *cup dry white wine*

Arrange the chicken breasts in one layer in a baking dish. Season with salt and pepper as desired and sprinkle with the tarragon. Whisk the lemon juice and wine together and pour over the chicken. Cover the pan with foil and bake in a 350°F oven for 35 minutes, or until the chicken is nearly done. Remove the foil and cook another 5 or 10 minutes, until the chicken turns golden brown. Transfer the chicken to a warm platter and pour about ½ cup of the cooking liquid over it.

Serves 4.

Classic Chicken with Tarragon. Serve this dish with lightly steamed vegetables and the pasta or grain of your choice.

Cinnamon-Spiced Chicken

This marinade has a simple but unusual blend of flavors. The results are delicious. Cornish game hens are tasty this way as well.

2   *small broiler/fryers, quartered*
1   *cup dry sherry*
1   *tablespoon ground cinnamon*
½   *cup honey*
¼   *cup freshly squeezed lime juice*
1   *large clove garlic, peeled and minced*
    Salt and freshly ground pepper to taste

Place the chicken in a bowl. Whisk all of the remaining ingredients together (be generous with the pepper) and pour over the chicken, turning to coat. Cover and refrigerate at least 8 hours.

Transfer the chicken to a baking dish large enough to hold it in one layer; reserve the marinade. Bake the chicken in a 350°F oven until tender, for 50 to 60 minutes, basting with the marinade and turning occasionally.

Serves 4 to 6.

Coq au Vin

Perhaps the ultimate chicken stew, *coq au vin* is traditionally made with a mature cock that lends it a wonderful rich flavor. If you do use an older bird, double the simmering time. Mature pheasant can also be prepared with this recipe.

For the marinade:
1½   *cups red wine*
1   *clove garlic, peeled and sliced*
1   *bay leaf*
1   *sprig rosemary*
2   *sprigs thyme*
6   *black peppercorns*
2   *tablespoons olive oil*

For the stew:
1   *chicken, about 4½ pounds, cut into serving pieces*
1   *tablespoon olive oil*
1   *tablespoon butter*
¼   *pound bacon, cut into 1-inch pieces*
18   *pearl onions, peeled*
½   *pound button mushrooms, sliced*
2½   *tablespoons flour*
1½   *cups chicken stock*
2   *cloves garlic, peeled and crushed*
1   *shallot, peeled and crushed*
    Salt and freshly ground pepper to taste
¼   *cup chopped fresh parsley*

Combine all the ingredients for the marinade in a saucepan, bring to a boil, reduce the heat, and simmer for 5 minutes. Let cool.

Place the chicken in a large bowl and pour the marinade over it; turn to coat. Cover and refrigerate at least 8 hours.

Remove the chicken from the marinade, strain the liquid, and reserve with the herbs. Heat the oil and butter in a heatproof casserole over medium heat. Add the bacon and cook until it is brown and crisp; remove and drain on paper towels. Add the chicken and brown on both sides (do this in batches if necessary). Remove the chicken and set aside. Add the onions and cook until lightly browned. Remove and set aside. Add the mushrooms and cook until just tender. Remove and set aside. Remove all but 2 tablespoons of fat from the casserole. Stir in the flour and cook, stirring constantly, until foaming. Stir in the reserved marinade, herbs, chicken stock, garlic, shallot, and salt and pepper as desired. Add the chicken pieces. Bring slowly to a boil and simmer over low heat (or in a 350°F oven) until the chicken is tender, 45 to 60 minutes.

Remove the chicken from the casserole and keep warm. Remove the herbs, garlic, and shallot with a slotted spoon and discard. Stir in the onions and cook until almost tender, about 10 minutes. Add the mushrooms and simmer a few minutes. Add the chicken and bacon and coat with the sauce; heat through and correct the seasoning. Serve from the casserole, garnishing each portion with parsley.

Serves 4.

The rich flavor of Coq au Vin, which requires a long marinade, is well worth the wait.

Chicken Marsala

This is an Italian classic—simple but wonderful.

4   *chicken breast halves, bone and skin removed*
     Flour for dredging
2   *tablespoons butter*
2   *tablespoons olive oil*
¾   *cup marsala wine*
⅓   *cup chicken stock*
2   *tablespoons softened butter*
     Freshly ground pepper to taste

Pound the chicken to flatten slightly. Dredge in flour and shake off any excess. Heat the butter and oil in a skillet until foaming, add the chicken, and cook for 3 minutes on each side. Stir in the marsala and simmer for 15 minutes, or until tender. Transfer the chicken to a serving platter and keep warm. Add the stock to the skillet, bring to a boil, and boil for 2 minutes. Remove from the heat, whisk in the softened butter, and season to taste with pepper. Pour the sauce over the chicken and serve at once.

Serves 4.

Simple Soy Chicken

If time permits, marinate the chicken before baking; if not, the soy has enough punch to flavor this dish even when you put it together just before it goes in the oven.

4   *chicken breast halves, skin removed if desired*
     Juice of 2 lemons
¼   *cup soy sauce*
2   *tablespoons mild-flavored oil*
1   *inch fresh ginger, peeled and minced*
4   *scallions, coarsely sliced*
1   *carrot, very finely sliced*

Place the chicken breasts in one layer in a baking dish. Whisk the lemon juice, soy sauce, and oil together, stir in the scallions and ginger, and pour over the chicken, turning to coat. Bake in a 350°F oven until the chicken is done, about 45 minutes, basting occasionally and adding the carrot for the last 5 minutes of baking time.

Serves 4.

40 Cloves of Garlic Chicken

Long, slow, covered cooking transforms the garlic in this dish to a gentle creamy paste and rids it of its (to some) alarming pungency. Traditionally, the garlic is left in its skin so each diner can squeeze the cloves onto bread; here it is peeled to be a little less messy. You can prepare it either way.

1   *broiler/fryer, 3½ to 4 pounds*
     Salt and freshly ground pepper to taste
2   *sprigs rosemary*
2   *sprigs thyme*
2   *sprigs parsley*
2   *tender stalks celery, with leaves*
¼   *cup olive oil*
40   *cloves garlic, peeled*
1   *cup white wine*

Season the chicken with salt and pepper as desired. Place half the herbs and one stalk of celery in the cavity, then truss the bird. Heat the oil in a deep, flameproof casserole and brown the chicken on all sides. Tie the remaining herbs and celery together and add with the wine to the casserole. Cover the casserole and bake in a 325°F oven for 90 minutes without peeking, then check for doneness. Replace the cover and continue to cook until tender. Transfer the chicken to a serving platter, surround with the garlic, and keep warm. Skim any fat from the cooking liquid, then spoon over the bird. Serve with warm slices of French bread.

Serves 3 to 4.

Chicken Marsala is an easy-to-prepare but elegant entree.

Chicken with Roasted Peppers

Roasted peppers give this dish a distinctive flavor. Serve it with pasta tossed with oil and Parmesan cheese.

2   *green peppers*
1   *broiler/fryer, 3½ to 4 pounds, cut into serving pieces*
       Freshly ground pepper
7   *tablespoons olive oil*
1   *onion, peeled and chopped*
2   *cloves garlic, peeled and crushed*
1   *tablespoon chopped fresh rosemary leaves*
6   *tomatoes, peeled and quartered*
1   *eggplant, thinly sliced*

Roast the peppers (right on the rack) in a 350°F oven until scorched, then rub off the skins, quarter, and seed them.

Season the chicken with the pepper. Heat 3 tablespoons of the oil in a flameproof casserole over medium high heat and brown the chicken on all sides. Remove from the pan and set aside. Lower the flame a little. Add the onion and garlic and cook for 3 minutes. Stir in the rosemary, peppers, and tomatoes and cook 3 more minutes. Add the chicken, cover, and simmer for about 40 minutes, or until tender, basting frequently.

Heat the remaining oil in a skillet and fry the eggplant slices until golden on both sides. Using a slotted spoon, arrange the chicken pieces, peppers, and eggplant on a serving platter, keep warm. Bring the sauce in the pan to a boil, and boil for about 3 minutes to thicken slightly. Spoon the sauce over the chicken and serve at once.

Serves 3 to 4.

Chicken Pot Pie with Herbed Biscuit Topping

Perhaps the ultimate comfort food. This is a basic recipe, but you can add other vegetables if you like—green or lima beans, corn kernels, mushrooms, or half a turnip.

For the filling:
4   *tablespoons butter*
4   *chicken breast halves, skin and bone removed, cut into bite-size pieces*
2   *medium potatoes, peeled and cut into ½-inch cubes*
1   *large onion, peeled and chopped*
2   *large carrots, cut into ½-inch cubes*
¼   *cup flour*
1   *cup dry white wine*
3   *cups hot chicken stock*
1   *cup cream*
3   *tablespoons tomato paste*
       Salt and freshly ground pepper to taste

For the topping:
2   *cups flour*
2   *teaspoons baking powder*
½   *teaspoon salt*
2   *tablespoons fresh or **2** teaspoons dried mixed herbs*
¼   *cup grated Parmesan cheese*
2   *tablespoons butter, chopped*
1   *cup milk*

Prepare the biscuit topping first. Mix the flour, baking powder, and salt together in a bowl, add the herbs and cheese, mix well. Work the butter into the mixture with your fingertips. Make a well in the center and add the milk, mixing quickly with a fork. Turn the dough onto a lightly floured surface and knead

briefly. Press into a round ¾ inch thick. Cut into 7 rounds with a biscuit cutter or small glass and let rest while you prepare the filling.

Heat the butter in a flameproof casserole over medium heat. Add the chicken and cook, stirring constantly, for 3 minutes. Add the potatoes, onions, and carrots, and cook, stirring constantly, for 7 minutes. Add the flour, and cook, stirring constantly, for 2 minutes. Stir in the wine, chicken stock, cream, and tomato paste. Cook until the liquid is hot, stirring occasionally. Season with salt and pepper if desired.

Top with the biscuits and bake in a 350°F oven for about 20 minutes, or until the biscuits are golden brown.

Serves 4.

Chicken Pot Pie almost always evokes memories of childhood. This version is topped with biscuits rather than pie crust.

Sweet and tart flavors mingle in Chicken Casserole with Dried Fruit.

Chicken Casserole with Dried Fruit

This casserole was inspired by the cuisine of the Middle East. Serve it with basmati rice cooked with a pinch of saffron. It is shown made with chicken wings; if you prefer, use 2 small cut-up chickens, or the parts of your choice.

12	*chicken wings dredged in flour*
3	*tablespoons olive oil*
2	*onions, peeled and sliced*
12	*new potatoes, scrubbed*
1	*cup chicken stock*
1	*cup unsweetened apple juice or cider*
½	*cup freshly squeezed lemon juice*
2	*tablespoons honey, more if desired*
½	*pound dried apricots*
½	*pound dried apples, chopped*
¼	*pound pitted prunes*
	Salt and freshly ground pepper to taste
12	*black olives*
1	*tablespoon fresh thyme leaves (lemon thyme if possible)*

Heat the oil in a flameproof casserole over medium heat, add the chicken, and cook for 8 minutes, or until golden on all sides (do this in batches if necessary). Remove chicken from pan and drain.

Add the onions and potatoes to the pan and cook over low heat until the onion softens, about 5 minutes. Stir in the stock, juices, and honey. Add the chicken and dried fruit and bring to a boil. Cover, reduce the heat, and simmer until the chicken is done, 20 to 40 minutes, depending upon size of pieces.

Taste the sauce and add more honey if it seems too tart, season with salt and pepper if desired. Stir in the olives and thyme and serve at once.

Serves 4 to 6.

DUCK

Ducks are waterfowl; they are distinguished by long bodies with relatively large frames and often have beautiful plumage. Throughout the world there are about a hundred varieties of wild and domesticated ducks; they range in weight from two-and-a-half to about nine pounds, depending upon breed and sex.

Each region of the world has its own preferred breed of domesticated duck. Among the oldest and most common are Pekin or Long Island, which were first bred by the Chinese more than two thousand years ago. These did not reach the West until late in the nineteenth century, although other breeds were raised in Europe (and brought to the New World) prior to that time. Pekin ducks are killed when they are seven to eight weeks old and weigh four to five pounds; they have a relatively high proportion of fat to meat. Muscovy ducks can weigh up to nine pounds and are stronger flavored and quite meaty and lean; they are sometimes crossbred with other types to minimize the strong fla-

vor. Mallards, Barbarie, Aylesbury, Nantais, and Rouennais are some other domesticated breeds.

Duck, or more accurately duckling, is available fresh year round in many groceries, and can often be found frozen. Ducks are raised in much the same way chickens are, with a company or cooperative hatching the eggs, contracting the growing to smaller farmers, and then processing the birds. Ducklings are fed a diet of grains and soybeans. They are somewhat more complicated to pluck than chickens, which makes duck processing more labor-intensive; otherwise there is little difference in the way they are handled or prepared for market. There is a demand for duck feathers and down and some producers clean these by-products and sell them to apparel and home furnishings manufacturers. Incidentally, duck tongues and feet are considered delicacies by the Chinese and these parts are sometimes exported to Asia.

Duck cuisine is permeated by fears of greasiness and skimpy flesh. Currently

breeders are researching ways to eliminate some of the fattiness common to domesticated ducks, as well as to increase the amount of meat on their frames; some results of these efforts are already in the market. You can expect some differences between brands, but on the whole, if you have not cooked a duck in some time, you may be pleasantly surprised by these advances. If properly cooked so the fat drains off, duck is a good source of protein and some vitamins and minerals. Though all duck meat is dark, it is lighter than the dark meat on chicken. Duck can be roasted or grilled, and if the fat is trimmed away, it can also be braised or casseroled; some people insist that Muscovy duck makes the best soup.

Domesticated ducks are characterized by the fatty layer under their skin, which keeps the flesh moist while it cooks. To avoid greasiness in the finished dish, the skin (but not the meat) should be pricked during cooking so that the fat can drain off. Some people suggest roasting a bird for about 20 minutes be-

fore stuffing—or baking the stuffing in a separate casserole—so that it will not absorb too much grease. As with most poultry, there are people who love the taste of the crispy skin. But there is no rule that says you have to eat it, and the fat content of the bird is considerably lower when the skin is removed.

Wild ducks are leaner than domesticated varieties and have a stronger flavor, which can be affected by what they have been eating. A gamey or fishy flavor can be countered if onions, herbs, or citrus fruits are placed inside them while roasting; these should be discarded before serving. Another way to minimize the gamey smell or flavor is to skin the duck before cooking. Because wild duck can be very lean, it is often barded (see *How to Bard*, page 108). To determine whether this is necessary, check to see if there is much of a fatty layer under the skin.

Once you master the proper techniques for successfully cooking duck, you will find that it is nearly as versatile as chicken. Duck is inherently flavorful and many people like it best simply roasted or grilled. It is often prepared with sweet, fruit-based glazes, but it is equally good with spices, herbs, or wine.

When planning portion size, remember that duck has less meat than chicken and allow about one-and-a-half pounds (or one-half to one whole domestic duck breast) per serving. As ducks vary greatly in size, you will have to use some judgment in determining how much to prepare. Bear in mind that wild birds are less meaty than domestic. Their legs may be tough or full of tendons and are not always eaten. Domestic duck is usually served well done, but aficionados prefer wild duck medium rare.

WHAT TO LOOK FOR IN THE MARKET

Ducks are available in many forms in most grocery stores. *Whole duckling*, with the giblets, is the most common. Some markets now sell duckling parts as well. These may include *whole breast*, with the bone in but without the wings; *boneless breast*; *duckling halves*; *breast quarters*, the breast split in half with the wings attached; or *breast and leg quarters*. As with chicken or turkey, the price of the cuts varies, with breast pieces being the most expensive. *Smoked duck* is also available in a variety of cuts: look for it in specialty shops or the gourmet section of the grocery. It is very good in salads and hors d'oeuvres.

HOW TO ROAST A WHOLE DUCK

Refer to *How To Stuff and Truss a Bird*, page 106, and *How To Roast a Whole Bird*, page 108. Preheat the oven to 450°F. Place the bird in the oven and reduce the temperature to 350°F. Roasting time for duck varies greatly with the type and size of the particular bird and the recipe, but in general allow 15 to 20 minutes a pound unstuffed, and 20 to 25 minutes a pound stuffed, depending upon size; check early for doneness. If you like, you can roast a duck for 20 to 30 minutes at 450°F before lowering the oven temperature, but allow less overall cooking time if you do this. Duck benefits from being turned while roasting. Allow the roast duck to rest about 15 minutes before carving.

COOKING TIMES FOR VARIOUS CUTS OF DUCK

Duck is available in assorted cuts; these can be cooked in most of the ways appropriate to chicken as long as you allow for their fattier nature. Cooking times will vary greatly with the type and size of the duck and preparation method, but in general allow about 1½ to 2 hours in a 350°F oven for a cut-up, bone-in, 5-pound duck, and about ½ hour for a boneless breast.

HOW TO BUY AND STORE POULTRY

FRESH POULTRY

Commercially raised poultry is inspected when it is processed. It may or may not be graded, but in general that sold in the grocery is of Grade A quality. Poultry processing includes rapid and thorough chilling and refrigerated shipping. Most fresh poultry reaches the market within three days of processing and is packaged with a *sell-by* date. If properly refrigerated, it should remain wholesome for two days past this date. However, poultry is difficult to keep fresh in a home refrigerator, and if you do not plan to cook it within two days of purchase, it is wise to freeze it. Giblets do not keep as well as poultry flesh and should be cooked the day of purchase.

Look for plump birds with smooth, unblemished skin in packages that are not torn. If buying birds that are not prepackaged, buy them from a reputable shop; do not accept a bird that has hard or scaly skin or an unpleasant odor. The package (or butcher) will indicate the size and therefore age of the bird (broiler, roaster, young, etc.), and the breastbone of a young bird will be flexible.

Keep poultry refrigerated until ready to prepare, but do allow it to reach room temperature before cooking, or recipe times and temperatures will not be accurate. The amount of time necessary for this depends on the size of the bird or pieces, but one hour is usually sufficient.

FROZEN POULTRY

The process by which poultry is commercially frozen is more rapid and deep than that possible in a home freezer and this usually assures that it stays thoroughly frozen during shipping. When buying frozen birds be sure that the package is completely sealed and not torn. Watch for signs of freezer burn—brownish areas on the skin—or pinkish ice crystals; these indicate that the bird has been partially defrosted at some point and is likely to be tough or stringy.

Poultry that is purchased frozen will keep up to a year in a home freezer, though it will probably taste best if used within six months. If you are freezing fresh poultry yourself, seal it in foil or freezer wrap. Keep young chickens up to nine months, older ones for no more than four. Keep ducks and turkeys for no more than six months. Always pack the giblets separately and use them within three months. Do not freeze stuffed birds; a home freezer does not chill quickly enough to safely preserve them.

There are three ways to safely defrost poultry: in the refrigerator, under cold running water, or in the microwave. In the refrigerator, allow four hours per pound and leave the bird in its wrapping; a turkey or goose can take three or four days. Under cold running water, allow one to two hours for a chicken and eight for a turkey, and leave the bird in its wrapping. Follow the manufacturer's directions to defrost poultry in the microwave. Never allow poultry to defrost at room temperature. If your bird has not completely defrosted on schedule in the refrigerator, you can finish the process under cold running water.

RECESSED

Rice Soup with Duck

This is a thin, mildly spiced Thai soup that, like its European chicken counterpart, is considered a cure-all for minor ailments. Serve it for lunch or a late supper.

For the soup:

⅔	cup rice (uncooked)
15	cups water (more as needed)
3	tablespoons vegetable oil
5	cloves garlic, finely chopped
4	inches fresh ginger root, peeled and finely sliced
1	duckling breast (about 1 pound), cut in bite-size pieces (skin and fat removed)
2	teaspoons white pepper
½	cup fish sauce (available at oriental grocers)
1	small onion, thinly sliced
3	tablespoons chopped fresh coriander leaves
2	large shallots, chopped

For the garnish:

Crispy fried noodles, fresh coriander, sliced chilies or peppers, or chopped shallots, as desired

Bring the rice and water to a boil and simmer slowly, uncovered, until the rice is soft. Add more water, if needed, to make 12 cups rice and stock. Keep hot.

Heat the oil in a skillet and stir-fry the garlic and ginger for about 2 minutes. Add the duck, pepper, and fish sauce, and stir-fry until duck is cooked. Then add with the onion to the rice and stock. Cook for 2 to 3 minutes. Just before serving, stir in the coriander and shallots. Serve with garnishes as desired.

Serves 8 to 10.

Summer Duckling Salad

The flowers not only make this salad a visual treat, they give it a subtle zest. If they are not in season, toss in a tablespoon of rinsed and drained capers; substitute sprigs of watercress for the leaves. Begin with grilled duck if possible, and discard any skin and fat that may remain.

For the salad:

3½	to 4 cups cooked duck, cut in bite-size pieces
1½	cups cooked mixed grains: wheat berries, wild rice, and bulgur, or as desired
¼	cup slivered almonds
4	scallions, finely chopped
1	tablespoon fresh rosemary leaves, finely chopped
	Salt and freshly ground pepper to taste
12	to 18 nasturtium leaves, rinsed and dried
12	nasturtium blossoms
12	small, simple marigold blossoms

For the vinaigrette:

1	tablespoon Dijon mustard
2	tablespoons white vinegar, preferably rosemary
6	tablespoons olive oil

Combine all the salad ingredients except the leaves and blossoms in a bowl. In a separate small jar or bowl, whisk the mustard into the vinegar till dissolved, then add the oil and mix well. Toss just enough of the dressing into the salad to coat lightly, cover, and chill for at least one hour. Remove from the refrigerator ½ hour before serving.

Rinse the flowers if necessary and gently pluck the petals from the marigolds. Test the seasoning of the salad, and adjust if desired. Toss half of the flowers into the salad, arrange on a serving dish or individual plates, and garnish with the remaining flowers. If you wish to serve on greens, choose those that are tender and mild; avoid arugula and radicchio, which will compete with the other flavors.

Serves 4.

Instead of nasturtiums, pansies and violas can be added to Summer Duckling Salad.

Cold Breast of Duck with Oriental Citrus Glaze

This is an elegant and rather unusual dish; serve it for a special brunch or luncheon.

For the duck:

	Juice of 3 lemons
	Juice of 3 limes
1	cup orange juice
1	cup honey
1	teaspoon hot bean paste
⅓	cup balsamic vinegar
¼	cup soy sauce
2	tablespoons chopped fresh ginger
4	large cloves garlic, crushed
2	cups chicken stock
¼	teaspoon oriental five-spice seasoning
8	whole boneless duck breasts

For the garnish:

3	oranges, thinly sliced
2	bunches scallions, cleaned and trimmed

Mix all of the ingredients except the duck and garnish in a large saucepan and set aside. Heat a skillet over high flame and place the duck in it skin-side down; brown for 5 to 7 minutes per side or until very brown (do this in batches if necessary). Add the browned duck to the saucepan with the other ingredients.

When all the duck has been added to the saucepan, stir it to mix, then bring to a boil over high heat, cover, reduce the heat, and simmer for 30 minutes. Arrange the duck on a platter and reserve. Increase the heat under the saucepan and boil the sauce to reduce by two-thirds, about 25 minutes; it should be syrupy. Pour the sauce over the duck, turning to coat well. Chill thoroughly and garnish with the orange slices and scallions before serving.

Serves 12.

Grilled Breast of Duckling and Raspberry Salad

This salad is full of beautiful colors and good tastes.

For the marinade and dressing:

1	teaspoon chopped fresh thyme leaves
1	teaspoon pink peppercorns, crushed
¼	cup raspberry vinegar
1	tablespoon Dijon mustard
½	cup safflower oil
¼	cup hazelnut oil
	Salt and freshly ground black pepper to taste
3	boneless duck breasts, halved and trimmed of excess fat

For the salad:

1	pound small white turnips, peeled and sliced into ¼-inch rounds
3	endives
½	pound mâche or tender Bibb lettuce
1	small head radicchio
1	pint fresh raspberries

Mix the thyme, peppercorns, vinegar, and mustard together in a small bowl, blending thoroughly with a whisk. Pour in the oils in a thin stream, whisking continuously till well emulsified. Add salt and freshly ground pepper to taste.

Reserve ¼ cup of the marinade to dress the salad.

With a small sharp knife, make 3 slashes in the skin of each breast half, being careful not to cut into the flesh. Place the breasts in a bowl large enough to hold them all and pour in the remaining marinade, turning duck to coat well. Cover and refrigerate at least 8 hours.

Place the turnips in boiling water and boil until crisp-tender, about 5 minutes. Drain and plunge in cold water, drain again, and chill in a plastic bag or covered bowl.

Pull the leaves from the endive, clean, and reserve in a plastic bag. Wash the mâche or lettuce and radicchio, dry, and tear into bite-size pieces; reserve in a plastic bag. Refrigerate the salad until ready to serve.

Place the duck on the hot grill, skin-side down. Cover and cook 7 to 10 minutes. Turn and cook another 7 to 10 minutes, or until the juices run clear when a skewer is inserted into the flesh. Transfer the cooked duck to a warm platter and let rest 5 minutes. Slice the breast halves on an angle into paper-thin slices, keeping the shape of the breast intact.

To serve, toss the mâche and radicchio in a large bowl with the remaining marinade, then place a small handful in the center of each plate. Arrange a few endive spears at the top of each plate and fan the slices of one duck breast half at the bottom. Arrange the turnip slices along the remaining edges of the salad and sprinkle raspberries over all.

Serves 6.

Cold Breast of Duck with Oriental Citrus Glaze.

Rosemary Grilled Duckling

This is a very simple and fat-free way to prepare duckling, which is delicious suffused with smoky rosemary flavor. Let the duck marinate for at least one hour at room temperature or all day in the refrigerator. You can use this technique and experiment with other herbs.

Note: If you do not have herbal vinegar on hand, place a generous sprig of the fresh herb in a pint bottle of white vinegar, place the open bottle in a pan of water, and simmer uncovered for 20 minutes.

2   *5-pound ducklings, split, preferably with breastbone, backbone, and rib cage removed*
1   *cup rosemary vinegar, or as needed*
10   *6-inch sprigs fresh rosemary, broken into small pieces*
     Salt and freshly ground pepper to taste

Cut the excess skin and as much fat as possible from the neck and tail ends of the split ducklings, and prick the remaining skin. Pour a little vinegar into the bottom of a roasting pan large enough to hold them in one layer (use two pans if necessary) and place the halves in it skin-side down. Sprinkle with the chopped rosemary and salt and pepper, if desired. Pour more vinegar over, cover, and let marinate until ready to grill, basting with the vinegar from time to time.

Place the duckling halves on the hot grill flesh-side down; cover and grill for 15 minutes. Prick the skin again, turn skin-side down, and continue to grill until done—35 to 45 minutes more.

Serves 4 to 6.

Roast Muscovy Duck with Mustard Leek Sauce

The tangy sauce is a zesty complement to the richly flavored duck.

Note: You can make enough broth for the sauce by simmering the neck and giblets with an onion, garlic clove, and pinch of thyme in 2 cups of water while the duck is roasting (remove the liver after about 20 minutes).

For the duck:
1   *Muscovy duck, about 6 pounds*
1   *onion*
1   *lemon, cut in half*
   Several sprigs fresh thyme
   Salt and freshly ground pepper to taste

For the sauce:
1¼   *cups stock, approximately*
2   *medium leeks, white parts only, cleaned and thinly sliced*
2   *cloves garlic, peeled and pressed*
1   *to **2** teaspoons herbes de Provence*
1   *cup dry white wine*
2   *tablespoons Dijon mustard*
   Salt and freshly ground pepper to taste

Preheat the oven to 450°F. Trim any fatty deposits from the duck's cavities. Season the cavities with salt and pepper, if desired, and place the onion, lemon halves, and thyme inside. Truss the duck, season with salt and pepper, and prick the skin with a fork. Place it on one side on a **V**-shaped rack in a roasting pan. Roast for 15 minutes, then turn the duck onto its other side, pricking the skin again, and roast for another 15 minutes. Lower the oven temperature to 350°F, turn the duck onto its breast, and roast for another 15 minutes. Turn the duck onto its back, and con-

tinue to roast, allowing about 15 minutes a pound overall, until done.

Meanwhile make the sauce: Bring the stock to a boil and simmer the leeks, garlic, and herbs in it for about 15 minutes. Stir in ¾ cup of the wine and the mustard, dissolved in a little stock; heat through and set aside. About 15 minutes before the duck is done, brush it with some of the sauce. Be careful not to let the liquid drip into the hot fat in the pan or it could splatter dangerously.

When the duck is done, remove it from the oven and set on a warm platter to rest for 15 to 20 minutes; brush again with the sauce. Dissolve the flour in about ¼ cup of stock, and stir the remaining wine into the sauce. Return the sauce to the heat. Simmer, stirring frequently, until the sauce begins to thicken. Add the salt and pepper and correct the seasonings. Serve the sauce over the carved duck, or pass separately.

Serves 4.

Rosemary Grilled Duckling, served with peppers and olives and homemade potato salad. Prepare any of the birds this way and you will have a delightful meal.

Baked Duck with Honey-Mint Glaze

Here is a lovely blend of flavors. Trim as much fat as possible from the duck, but indulge yourself and leave the skin over the flesh to crisp.

1   duck (about 5½ pounds), butterflied
¼   cup honey
1   tablespoon fresh thyme leaves
4   tablespoons chopped fresh mint leaves
½   teaspoon cinnamon
2   lemons
8   cloves

Mix the honey, thyme, mint, and cinnamon in a small saucepan. Add the juice of the lemons, reserve the peel. Heat just enough to dissolve and stir to mix. Quarter the lemon peel and stick a clove into each piece; add half to the mixture. Let cool.

Prick the skin of the duck liberally, then place it skin-side down on a lightly oiled flat rack in a roasting pan (use the broiler pan from your oven). Brush the honey sauce over the duck, turn, and brush the other side. Scatter the remaining lemon peel over. Cover loosely and let stand for 2 hours. Reserve the rest of the sauce.

Turn the duck skin-side down on the pan, place in a 400°F oven, and bake for about 25 minutes. Then turn and brush the duck from time to time with the remaining glaze until done, about 25 minutes more; it should be dark and crispy.

Serves 3–4.

Summer-Berry Breast of Duckling with Zucchini Blossoms

Here duckling breasts are cooked in a slightly spiced sweet-sour sauce and served with batter-dipped blossoms. Though blueberries are indicated, you can cook the duck in any seasonal berry.

For the duck:
3   tablespoons mild vegetable oil
4   small whole boneless duckling breasts
4   tablespoons balsamic vinegar
      Freshly ground black pepper
¼   teaspoon cinnamon
⅓   cup fresh blueberries

For the zucchini:
¾   cup flour
1   cup water
      Oil for frying
12   zucchini blossoms

Trim any excess fat from the duck. Heat the oil in a skillet and cook the duck, skin-side down, over low heat until skin is golden. Turn and cook the other side.

Add the vinegar, pepper to taste, cinnamon, and berries. Cover and cook over low heat until duck is tender, about 15 minutes.

Meanwhile, prepare the flowers. Gradually sift the flour into the water and mix with a fork to make a smooth batter; if necessary, add more water. When the duck is nearly done, pour about 1 inch of oil into a skillet and heat until very hot. Dip the blossoms into the batter and fry a few at a time until golden.

Serve the duck drizzled with the sauce and accompanied by the blossoms.

Serves 4.

Many-Splendored Duck

Although it seems that there is a plethora of garlic and ginger in this recipe, they simply infuse the duck with flavor while it simmers slowly, and are then discarded.

Note: If you use a larger duckling, cut it in half or increase the cooking time somewhat. Use a saucepan that is just large enough to hold the duck.

¼   pound fresh ginger
1   head garlic
1   small duckling (3 pounds)
2   cups water
¼   cup soy sauce
⅓   cup honey

Peel the ginger, then pound lightly with a mallet or rolling pin; cut into ½-inch chunks. Pound garlic lightly and remove skins.

Place the ginger and garlic in a heavy saucepan with the duck and water. Bring to a boil, add the soy sauce, return to a boil, cover, reduce the heat, and simmer gently for 2 hours, turning once after 75 minutes. Remove the duck from the pan; strain and reserve the liquid, discarding fat, garlic, and ginger.

Return the liquid and duck to the pan and bring to a boil. Pour the honey over the duck, reduce the heat, and simmer uncovered for 30 minutes, basting frequently.

Remove the duck from the pan and cut into bite-size pieces, and arrange on a serving platter. Bring the sauce back to a boil and pour over duck.

Serves 2.

Baked Duck with Honey-Mint Glaze is lightly spiced with cinnamon and cloves.

Cranberry Apple Braised Duck

The duck and sauce are cooked together for a melding of sweet-sour flavors. If the results are too tart for your taste, add a little honey or brown sugar at the end.

1 duck, about 5 pounds
   Salt and freshly ground pepper to taste
1 tablespoon butter
1½ cups fresh cranberries, mixed with 2 apples, cored and diced
½ cup cider or apple juice
1 cup broth

Trim any excess skin and fat from the duck's cavities. Prick the skin, season with salt and freshly ground pepper as desired, and truss. Melt the butter in a flameproof heavy casserole in a 425°F oven. Place the duck on one side (leg) in the casserole and roast uncovered for 15 minutes. Turn to the other side and roast another 15 minutes. Reduce the oven temperature to 375°F. Lift the duck from the casserole and discard the fat. Add about ⅓ of the cranberry-apple mix and the cider to the casserole, and place the duck in it breast-side down. Roast for 20 minutes; turn onto its back and roast another 20 minutes or until done. Transfer the duck to a platter and keep warm.

Add the broth to the casserole and bring to a boil on the stovetop, stirring frequently. Simmer to mix the flavors

Prepare Cranberry Apple Braised Duck on a gloomy autumn day when the fruit is in season and your spirits need an aromatic, colorful lift.

and reduce if it is very thin. Strain the broth, pressing the liquid from the fruit; discard the fruit and skim the fat from the broth. Return the broth to the casserole and stir in the remaining fruit; bring to a simmer. Remove the trussing from the duck, return it to the casserole, and simmer for about 10 minutes, or until the fruit is just soft. Transfer the duck to a serving platter, spoon a little of the fruit over it. Serve the remaining sauce separately.

Serves 3 to 4.

Tagliatelle with Duck Liver Cream Sauce

This is a very easy and very rich dish. Consider serving it as a first course. Start with good quality pâté—choose one flavored with green peppercorns or a liqueur, if you like—and be ready to work quickly, as you should make the sauce while the pasta is cooking.

1 pound fresh tagliatelle or fettuccine
1 cup light or medium cream
½ pound duck liver pâté
   Salt and freshly ground pepper to taste
1 tablespoon walnut oil
1 tablespoon chopped chives or 1 teaspoon fresh thyme leaves
2 tablespoons finely chopped walnuts

   Grated Parmesan cheese for garnish

Put the pasta on to cook; place the cream and pâté in a small saucepan over medium heat and stir constantly until the pâté is melted and you have a thick sauce. Season with salt and pepper as desired. Keep warm.

Drain the pasta when it is al dente, and toss with the oil in a serving bowl. Stir the herbs and walnuts into the sauce and toss it in with the pasta. Serve sprinkled with Parmesan cheese.

Serves 4 to 6 as a first course, 3 to 4 as a main course.

GOOSE

Goose, like turkey, is traditionally a holiday bird. Like ducks, geese are waterfowl with large frames and fatty skin. Geese have been domesticated for thousands of years, but it is unclear exactly when they were first raised for their meat. It is known that in ancient Roman times geese guarded the temples of the goddess Juno; however, the Romans did not eat them, thinking their flesh too dry. The Gauls fattened and ate geese, and when invaded by the Romans, shared their culinary knowledge. By the Middle Ages goose had become a very popular meat and large flocks of them were common. Geese are still common in Europe, but in North America they are generally available only at holiday times or by special order.

Domestic geese are killed before they are a year old and weigh between 6 and 14 pounds when dressed. If you have ever seen one in a farmyard, you will be aware that they seem quite large and aggressive when alive. Goose is high in protein and iron, but also higher in fat than other poultry. The meat is dark with a rich flavor and moist and tender,

if somewhat stringy. If one can make such a culinary comparison, it falls somewhere between turkey and lamb in flavor and texture. Goose should be prepared for roasting like duck: the skin should be pricked so the fat can drain; domestic goose is too fatty to be suitable for braising. Between their fat and their large frames, they do not yield the quantity of meat you might expect, so allow 2 pounds per serving. In addition to whole goose, *goose breast*, with or without the bone, and *smoked goose* are available from specialty food shops or mail-order sources.

Wild geese such as the Canada goose, white-fronted goose, snow goose, and brant are neither as large nor as fatty as their domesticated counterparts. They are also not as tender. Only young wild geese (no more than 5 pounds dressed) should be roasted (be sure to bard them) or grilled; older ones can be braised. Sportsmen say they are delicious as long as they have not been eating fish, which gives the meat a fishy taste.

HOW TO ROAST A WHOLE DOMESTIC GOOSE

Refer to *How to Stuff and Truss a Bird*, page 106, and *How to Roast a Whole Bird*, page 108. Remove all excess fat from the cavities and be sure to prick the skin on the back as well as the breast and legs. Plan to roast for 15 minutes a pound unstuffed, 20 minutes a pound stuffed. Preheat the oven to 400°F and roast the goose for about one-third of the calculated period, then reduce the temperature to 325°F for the remainder. It is very helpful to use a meat thermometer when cooking a goose, because the fat that drains is clear and can easily be confused with the juices when checking for doneness. Be sure to drain the excess fat from the

Whole Roast Goose often graces dinner tables in Europe; here it is unfortunately the exception rather than the rule. It is really no more trouble to prepare than any other roast bird—just be careful of the hot fat.

pan at least every half hour—there could be as much as a quart. Be very careful, as the fat will be very hot and could cause a bad burn. If possible, use a metal-tubed bulb-syringe, as a plastic one is likely to melt; otherwise use a metal spoon. Be sure your hands and the utensil are dry, and don't tip the goose so that juice from the cavity drains into the pan because liquid hitting the hot fat will cause it to splatter. Let the roast goose rest 20 to 30 minutes before carving.

Goose can be stuffed with a bread- or rice-based stuffing, to which onions, chestnuts, tart fruit, or a combination can be added; refer to the chapters on chicken and turkey for basic stuffing recipes. Many people like to add sausage to the stuffing, but as goose is already so high in fat, this makes a very rich meal. Another traditional stuffing is made from mashed potatoes (recipe below).

Goose fat is considered a flavorful— though hardly low-cholesterol—cooking fat by many, and there is likely to be a considerable amount of it inside the body cavity. To render it for later use, cut it from the cavity, chop it, and cook in a heavy skillet or saucepan with a little water until it is melted. Cool slightly, then strain through a sieve lined with cheesecloth to remove any fibers. It will keep in the refrigerator for 2 to 3 months.

The medley of flavors in Salad of Goose with Green Peppercorns, Goat Cheese, and Sun-Dried Tomatoes is complemented by a light, fresh garnish of lemon and cucumbers.

STORING AND REHEATING COOKED BIRDS

Always refrigerate leftover birds as soon as you know they are leftover; never let them sit at room temperature for more than two hours. You can safely keep a cooked bird in the refrigerator for two days. If stuffed, remove the stuffing and store it in a separate container. Seal the bird in plastic wrap or place it in a covered container. If you will not be using the bird that quickly, freeze it.

Since poultry tends to dry out, it is best to reheat it covered, with some liquid in the pan. If you wish to reheat a roasted bird, bring it to room temperature, cover it loosely with foil, and place in a 325°F oven until heated through. The time will depend upon the size of the bird, but it could take almost as long to reheat as a bird of comparable size would to cook originally, and could dry out in the process. It is preferable to remove the meat from the carcass and heat it in a covered casserole, or use it in a recipe calling for cooked poultry (or whatever bird you have). If you are reheating gravy or any sauce made with meat stock, always bring it to the boiling point. As most game birds are small and either rare or expensive, it is unlikely that you will be faced with many leftovers, but they, like most poultry, can be used imaginatively in salads or sandwiches.

RECIPES

Salad of Goose with Green Peppercorns, Goat Cheese, and Sun-Dried Tomatoes

Trim all remaining fat from the cooked meat. Serve with fresh bread and cornichons.

½	cup sun-dried tomatoes, marinated in a little olive oil
6	to 8 fresh basil leaves, chopped
2	tablespoons drained green peppercorns
2	cups cooked goose, in bite-size pieces
¼	pound semi-soft goat cheese, crumbled
	Assorted fresh salad greens (about 4 cups), washed and dried

For the vinaigrette:

1	teaspoon Dijon mustard
2	tablespoons balsamic vinegar
6	tablespoons olive oil

If your sun-dried tomatoes are not marinated, blanch them briefly in boiling water, drain, and toss with a little olive oil. Add the basil to the tomatoes. Crush the peppercorns in a mortar or with the back of a spoon. In a small jar or bowl, whisk the mustard into the vinegar till dissolved, then add the oil and mix well. Mix the goose, tomatoes, and peppercorns in a bowl, toss with enough of the vinaigrette to coat lightly, cover, and refrigerate for at least an hour to blend the flavors. Remove from the refrigerator ½ hour before serving.

Toss the greens with some of the vinaigrette and arrange them on a serving platter or individual plates. Top with the goose salad. Crumble the cheese over all.

Serves 4.

Roast Goose with Mint Pesto

The rich flavor of the goose—with or without gravy—is nicely countered by this slightly piquant condiment. Think of serving this in early summer or fall—fresh mint is essential. Should you have any leftovers, or if the weather is hot, serve the goose cold and sliced thin, and garnish with the pesto.

For the goose:
1 *10-to-12-pound goose, or size desired*
   Salt and freshly ground pepper to taste
12 *to **14** pearl onions, peeled*
   Generous sprigs of fresh herbs, about 2 cups total—rosemary, sorrel, parsley, thyme

For the mint pesto:
½ *cup olive oil*
2 *cups fresh mint leaves*
½ *cup fresh parsley leaves*
1 *large shallot, peeled and coarsely chopped*
½ *cup broken walnuts*
   Juice of ½ lime

Refer to *How to Roast a Whole Domestic Goose*, page 60. Season the goose with salt and pepper as desired. Put the onions and herbs in the cavity and truss. Roast as described.

Place about ¼ cup of oil in the container of a food processor. Add all the other ingredients except the lime juice and process to chop fine. Add the rest of the oil and the lime juice and process to mix.

Discard the herbs from the cavity. Carve the goose and garnish each portion with the pearl onions and a small dollop (a soupspoonful) of pesto.

Serves 5 to 7; makes about 1½ cups pesto.

Roast Goose with Mint Pesto.

Mashed Potato Stuffing

Mashed potatoes are a traditional stuffing for goose. Here they are seasoned with rosemary and garlic, but you can use herbs of your choice and omit the garlic if you like.

5   *cups boiled, peeled, and mashed potatoes*
3   *cloves garlic, peeled and crushed*
4   *tablespoons fresh rosemary leaves, minced*
1½ *cups yogurt or sour cream*
2   *eggs beaten*
2   *cups fresh bread crumbs, more if needed*
    Salt and freshly ground pepper to taste

Mix all of the ingredients together, adding the bread crumbs last and mixing to make a fairly stiff mélange. Season with salt and pepper to taste.

Makes about 8 cups stuffing.

 # GROUSE

Grouse is an upland game bird that is native to the Northern Hemisphere. There are many varieties, including sage grouse, ruffed grouse, snow grouse, blue, red, and black grouse, greater and lesser prairie chicken, and willow, rock, and white-tailed ptarmigan. They are all ground-grazing birds that live primarily in woods, thickets, and areas of semi-dense underbrush; the sage grouse lives in sage brush countryside and the blue grouse on tree-covered mountain slopes. The various types eat insects, leaves, buds, seeds, grasses, acorns, and/or berries, and their flesh is flavored by their diet. The sage grouse is the largest upland game bird after the wild turkey and looks a bit like a pheasant; hunters recommend eviscerating it immediately after killing to prevent it from absorbing the bitter flavor of the sage it eats. Some grouse are farmed but most are found in the wild.

When dressed, grouse vary in size from about one-half to three pounds; it is usual to serve one per person, but that may vary with the type and size available. Grouse have red flesh that is not unlike red meat in taste and they are very lean. They are best when young. If barded, they can be roasted or grilled; otherwise—or if over six months old—they should be braised or casseroled so as not to dry out.

HOW TO ROAST A WHOLE GROUSE

Refer to *How to Stuff and Truss a Bird*, page 106, *How to Bard*, page 108, and *How to Roast a Whole Bird*, page 108. Grouse is a very lean bird, so be sure to bard it, or bake covered, or cook with moisture. There is quite a variation in size and flavor among the many kinds of grouse, few of which are farmed, so suggested cooking times should be taken as estimates only. Grouse and partridge are often cooked interchangeably, so refer to the partridge chapter for additional recipes, remembering that small grouse may not require as much cooking time as partridge. If you wish to roast it uncovered, bard well and baste frequently. Preheat the oven to 450°F, place the bird in it, and reduce the temperature to 350°F. Roast for 20 minutes per pound unstuffed, 25 minutes per pound stuffed, but check early for doneness. If the bird weighs less than one pound, it will probably take at least 30 minutes to cook. If you like, you can roast grouse at a higher temperature (400°F) for some or all of the cooking period, but allow less time overall. Let rest for 5 to 10 minutes before carving or serving.

Roast Grouse with Mushroom Sauce

The earthiness of mushrooms complements the gamey taste of the grouse. If you would prefer a richer sauce, stir in 1 cup of sour cream at the end and heat through but do not boil.

4 *grouse, about 12 ounces each, or as needed for 4 people*
2 *lemons, halved*
4 *teaspoons green peppercorns, drained*
Barding fat

For the sauce:
2 *tablespoons butter*
4 *shallots, peeled and chopped*
2 *teaspoons fresh thyme leaves*
1 *tablespoon flour*
1 *cup chicken stock*
¾ *pound mushrooms, cleaned and thinly sliced*
¼ *cup dry sherry*
Salt and freshly ground pepper to taste

Refer to *How to Roast a Whole Grouse*, page 65. Place a lemon half and a teaspoon of green peppercorns in the cavity of each bird, bard, and truss. Place in a 400°F oven and roast until tender, 25 to 30 minutes.

To make the sauce, melt one tablespoon of the butter in a saucepan over medium heat, add the shallots and thyme, and cook, stirring, for 3 minutes. Stir in the flour and blend well. Add the stock slowly, stirring constantly. Leave on very low heat while you cook the mushrooms. Melt the remaining butter in a large skillet over medium heat. Add the mushrooms, and cook over high heat, stirring frequently, until they release their liquid and are firm and golden brown. (If your skillet is not large enough to cook the mushrooms without crowding them, cook in batches.) Add to the pan with the stock and simmer for about 15 minutes. Just before serving, add the sherry, bring to a boil, and season with salt and pepper to taste.

Cut the grouse in half if desired, place on a serving platter, and drizzle with some of the sauce. Pass the rest of the sauce at the table.

Serves 4; makes about 2 cups of sauce.

Roast Grouse with Mushroom Sauce.

Grouse Braised with Fennel and Raisins

Here is a wonderfully easy way to make a dish with a sophisticated flavor.

4   *grouse, about 12 ounces each, halved*
       Salt and freshly ground pepper to taste
3   *tablespoons olive oil*
2   *fennel bulbs, trimmed and cut into thick slices*
2   *shallots, peeled and minced*
½   *cup raisins*
       Grated rind of 1 small orange
1   *cup chicken stock*
1   *cup red wine*

Season the grouse with salt and pepper if desired. Put the olive oil in a baking dish large enough to hold the grouse in one layer (or divide between two dishes). Add the fennel, shallots, raisins, and orange rind, and stir around to mix; then spread in a layer over the bottom. Arrange the grouse on top. Pour half the stock and half the wine over the dish's contents, cover with foil, and bake in a 350°F oven until the birds are tender, about one hour. Check from time to time; if the liquid cooks away, add more. Serve from the baking dish.

Serves 4.

Grouse Braised with Fennel and Raisins is twice delightful—aromatic while simmering and delicious at the table.

GUINEA FOWL

Guinea fowl are native to the west coast of Africa. They were eaten by pre-Christian Greeks and Romans but, with the fall of the Roman Empire, disappeared from Europe until the Portuguese reintroduced them in the sixteenth century. Most are wild or free-range farmed. Occasionally you see them in farmyards, where they are noticeable for their white-spotted gray plumage and pheasantlike stance.

Guinea fowl have both light and dark meat and are very lean, so bard them before roasting. Recipes for pheasant and most chicken recipes can be used for them; just take care to keep the birds from drying out. They are delicious served cold as well as hot. If young—one to two pounds dressed—they can be roasted, grilled, or broiled; adults—two to three pounds—can be roasted, braised, or casseroled. One guinea fowl will serve 2 to 3 people.

HOW TO ROAST A WHOLE GUINEA FOWL

Refer to *How to Stuff and Truss a Bird*, page 106, *How to Bard*, page 108, and *How to Roast a Whole Bird*, page 108. Preheat the oven to 450°F, place the bird in it, and reduce the temperature to 350°F. Roast for 20 minutes a pound unstuffed, 25 minutes a pound stuffed, but check early for doneness. Allow to rest about 10 minutes before carving.

A WORD ON AGING GAME BIRDS

Game birds must be aged to become tender, and to improve their flavor if young. This is done by hanging them by the feet or head at least until the rigor mortis passes. The period of hanging varies with the size and age of the bird, weather conditions, and the tradition of the producer or hunter and the country; it can range from one day to two weeks. Birds must be hung in cool dry places where the air can circulate freely. They are hung in their feathers but may or may not be eviscerated. The longer a bird hangs, the more tender it will be; older birds therefore require longer hanging. Many hunters say that the longer a bird has hung, the more delicious it is, while admitting that they are reluctant to hang birds themselves for any great length of time. In France it is traditional to hang birds by their heads until they drop (or nearly do) of their own weight and the odor can be marked. Hunters leave game birds in the feather until they are to be prepared for cooking; they can be frozen that way. Smaller game birds are sometimes cooked with the *trail* (viscera) still in place. If you are not supplied with game birds by a sportsperson, you will find them at specialty shops or through mail-order suppliers, either fresh or frozen; these may also include the trail.

RECIPES

Herb-and-Tomato Braised Guinea Fowl

This is a marvelously scented mélange. Make it on a rainy day in summer when all the ingredients are fresh, or use canned tomatoes in the winter. Try this with a simple whole-grain pilaf—bulgur, millet or kasha, or polenta.

3	tablespoons olive oil
2	guinea fowl, quartered
4	leeks, trimmed, cleaned, and sliced
6	cloves garlic
8	medium-size ripe tomatoes, peeled and cut in chunks
½	cup dry white wine
3	lemons
½	cup chopped fresh basil leaves
½	cup chopped fresh coriander leaves
¼	cup chopped fresh parsley
2	tablespoons chopped fresh tarragon Salt and freshly ground pepper to taste

Heat the oil in a flameproof casserole and brown the fowl on both sides in

Lemons, tomatoes, and intensely flavored herbs infuse this Herb-and-Tomato Braised Guinea Fowl with freshly scented flavors.

batches. Remove from the casserole, lower the heat, and stir in the leeks. Crush the garlic in a press and add to the casserole; sauté for about 5 minutes. Add the fowl. Cover and simmer over low heat for 20 minutes; do not lift the lid.

Mix the tomatoes and wine in a bowl. Grate the lemon rind, mix with half the herbs. Cover and reserve. Squeeze the lemon juice into the tomatoes and stir in the remaining herbs. Add to the casserole, stirring to mix well. Cover and continue to simmer until the fowl is tender,

about 35 minutes. Stir in the remaining herbs with the lemon peel, simmer briefly to release the flavors, season with salt and pepper, if desired, and serve immediately.

Serves 4 to 6, depending on size of fowl.

Coriander Grilled Guinea Fowl

The piquant marinade and the grilling are a lovely complement to this full-flavored fowl.

For the marinade:
3   tablespoons olive oil
¼   cup white vinegar
6   tablespoons fresh coriander leaves
2   cloves garlic

2   guinea fowl, about 2½ pounds each, halved, preferably with backbone, breastbone, and rib cage removed
Salt and freshly ground pepper to taste

Mix the oil and vinegar in a small bowl. Peel the garlic and press it; stir into the oil and vinegar with the coriander leaves. Season the fowl with salt and pepper, if desired, and arrange them in a large shallow pan. Pour the marinade over them and turn them to coat well. Cover the pan and refrigerate for at least 8 hours.

Place the fowl skin-side up on a hot grill, cover, and cook for 15 minutes. Turn them and continue to cook until done, about 45 minutes more, or until the juices run clear when a skewer is inserted into the flesh.

Serves 4.

Roast Guinea Fowl with Lemon, Thyme, and Parsley Stuffing

This very simple, fragrant stuffing is a lovely complement to the full flavor of the fowl.

Note: To make your own bread crumbs, toast slices of bread in a very low oven until dry, not brown, and crush with a rolling pin; 8 to 10 slices should suffice, depending on loaf size.

For the stuffing:
6   tablespoons butter
1   onion, peeled and chopped
3   cups fresh whole-grain bread crumbs
2   tablespoons fresh lemon thyme leaves
⅓   cup chopped fresh parsley
Grated rind of 1 lemon
1   egg, beaten with 1 tablespoon stock or water
Salt and freshly ground pepper to taste

For the guinea fowl:
2   guinea fowl, about 2½ pounds
Salt and freshly ground pepper to taste
Barding fat

Refer to *How to Roast a Whole Guinea Fowl*, page 68. Melt the butter in a skillet and sauté the onions until transparent, about 5 minutes. Mix the bread crumbs and herbs in a bowl; add the on-

ions, butter, and lemon rind. Mix thoroughly, then mix in the egg. Season with salt and pepper as desired.

Preheat the oven to 450°F. Season the guinea fowl with the salt and pepper, if desired. Stuff each bird loosely, truss, bard, and place on a rack in roasting pan. Place in the oven and roast for 10 minutes; lower the heat to 350°F and continue to cook until done, about 60 minutes, or until the juices run clear when a skewer is inserted into the flesh; baste from time to time and remove the barding fat for the last 20 minutes so the birds can brown.

Remove the trussing strings, spoon the stuffing into a serving bowl, and halve, quarter, or carve the birds as you wish.

Serves 4.

Homemade whole-grain bread crumbs and fresh herbs complement Roast Guinea Fowl with Lemon, Thyme, and Parsley Stuffing.

Guinea Fowl Braised with Caraway Cabbage

If you like cabbage, this is a wonderful winter meal. Older birds benefit from slow covered cooking of this sort. If you like, tuck some small sausages into the cabbage during the last 10 minutes of cooking.

1	*head cabbage*
2	*tablespoons mild-flavored oil or butter*
1	*3½-pound or* **2** *2½-pound guinea fowl, trussed*
2	*onions, peeled and thinly sliced*
2	*tablespoons caraway seed*
1	*bunch baby carrots, scrubbed*
	Salt and freshly ground pepper to taste
12	*juniper berries*
2	*cups stock*
½	*cup white wine*
	Fresh parsley or thyme for garnish

Cut the cabbage in quarters and discard the core. Steam the quarters for 5 to 8 minutes, or until somewhat softened. Let cool enough to handle, separate the leaves, and place in a large bowl.

Heat the oil in a flameproof casserole and brown the guinea fowl on all sides. Remove from the casserole, lower the heat, add the onions, and sauté until wilted. Add the onions to the cabbage with the caraway seeds and toss to mix, seasoning with salt and pepper if desired. Scatter the juniper berries on the bottom of the casserole. Place half the cabbage mix in the casserole, add the guinea fowl, and arrange the carrots around it. Cover with the rest of the cabbage. Pour in the stock and wine, cover the casserole, and simmer over low heat for 60 to 75 minutes, or until tender.

When done, remove the carrots and guinea fowl from the casserole, and cut into serving pieces if desired. Transfer the cabbage to a colander with a slotted spoon and let drain. Arrange the cabbage on a serving platter, top with the guinea fowl and carrots; cover and place in a warm oven. Strain the cooking liquid into a small saucepan, skim off any fat, and boil to reduce somewhat; adjust the seasoning if desired. Pour some of this sauce over the fowl and cabbage and sprinkle parsley or thyme on top. Serve, passing the rest of the sauce separately.

Serves 3 to 4.

Guinea Fowl Braised with Caraway Cabbage.

Partridge are upland game birds that are highly prized by sportsmen. They are a bit larger than quail, weighing about three-quarters of a pound dressed, and have plump legs. There are several varieties of partridge, both wild and farmed; they live in open, barren environments and eat insects, seeds, grasses, and other vegetation. True partridges are not native to the Western Hemisphere, although some grouse are often referred to as partridge. Chukar (from the Himalayas) and Hungarian partridge were brought from Europe to the United States in the late nineteenth century.

Partridge is very flavorful; it is lean and should be barded before roasting. It can also be grilled or braised and cooked following recipes for grouse or Cornish game hen; it is chewy and benefits from longer, slower cooking. It is usual to serve one per person. *Smoked partridge* is available from specialty food shops.

HOW TO ROAST A WHOLE PARTRIDGE

Refer to *How to Stuff and Truss a Bird*, page 106, *How to Bard*, page 108, and *How to Roast a Whole Bird*, page 108. Partridge is a chewy bird. It is most successfully cooked covered so that it steams rather than roasts. To do this, bard and truss the birds, place in a casserole with a tight lid or wrap in foil, and bake in a 325°F oven for at least one hour. If you wish to roast it uncovered, bard well, baste frequently, and plan to cook longer than you might expect for the size. Preheat the oven to 450°F, place the bird in it, and reduce the temperature to 350°F. Roast for 40 minutes unstuffed, 45 to 50 minutes stuffed, but check early for doneness. Let rest for 5 minutes before serving. Partridge and grouse are often cooked interchangeably, so you can refer to the grouse chapter for additional recipes, remembering that you may have to increase the cooking time.

RECIPES

Partridge Romaine

This is a tender way to prepare small birds without barding them. There is an element of pleasant surprise when the singed leaves are peeled from the mound to reveal the succulent treasure within.

Note: Use a generous roasting pan for this so that you can build a mound of lettuce over the birds without it spilling over the edges.

1	*large head Romaine lettuce, leaves separated and washed*
4	*onions, peeled and thinly sliced*
1	*can plum tomatoes, drained and thinly sliced*
2	*teaspoons minced fresh fennel leaves*
2	*cloves garlic, peeled and minced*
1	*lemon, quartered*
4	*partridges, 12 ounces each*
½	*cup olive oil, or as needed*
	Salt and freshly ground pepper to taste

Select the 12 largest lettuce leaves and put them in a bowl of hot water. Cut the rest crosswise into strips about 1 inch wide. Brush the bottom of the roasting pan with oil. Spread half the cut lettuce in it, followed by half the onions, half the tomatoes, half the fennel, and half the garlic. Drizzle with a little oil and season with a grind of pepper.

Place a lemon quarter in each bird and truss. Heat 3 tablespoons of the oil in a skillet and brown the birds on all sides. Season with salt and pepper if desired and arrange them close together with breasts up on the bed of lettuce.

Drizzle with a little oil, then top with the remaining vegetables *in reverse order* from garlic to lettuce. Drizzle with a little oil. Drain the large lettuce leaves and cover the mound completely with them; pour the remaining oil over all.

Place in a 350°F oven and bake for 60 to 75 minutes, or until tender. Remove the outer leaves if they are charred and serve the birds with the vegetables from the baking dish.

Serves 4.

For Partridge Romaine, birds are buried in a mound of greens for a slow bake; they emerge moist and succulent.

Braised Partridge with Lentils

The French claim to grow the best lentils; this dish is a classic of that country. Though not necessarily part of the tradition, either millet or polenta makes a good companion dish.

For the partridge:

½	pound thickly sliced bacon, cut in 1-inch pieces
4	partridges, 12 ounces each, trussed
2	onions, peeled and chopped
3	sprigs each thyme and rosemary, tied together with string
1	cup white wine
3	cups stock

For the lentils:

2	cups lentils, washed and picked over
1	small onion, peeled
3	cloves garlic, peeled
4	cups water or stock, more if needed
2	teaspoons fresh thyme leaves
2	carrots, diced
2	tablespoons vinegar, preferably thyme
	Salt and freshly ground pepper to taste

Brown the bacon over medium heat in a flameproof casserole large enough to hold the birds in one layer. Remove the bacon pieces from the pan and brown the partridges on all sides in the fat. Add the onion and cook until transparent. Return the bacon to the pan and add the remaining ingredients. Cover and simmer over low heat for 75 to 90 minutes, or until tender, turning the birds occasionally.

When the partridges have been simmering for about 50 minutes, start the lentils. Place them in a saucepan with the onion, garlic, and water, bring to a boil, cover, reduce the heat, and simmer for 10 minutes. Add the carrots and thyme without stirring. Cover and cook until the lentils are just barely tender, about 10 minutes more; if necessary, add more liquid. Remove from the heat, discard the onion and garlic, and stir in the vinegar; season with salt and pepper, if desired.

When the partridges are done, remove them from the casserole and discard the trussing; halve them if desired. Strain the cooking liquid, discard the bunch of herbs, and skim off the fat; return ¼ inch of the liquid to the casserole and reserve the rest in a saucepan. Add the lentils to the casserole along with the bacon and onion, stir to mix, and add the partridges. Cover and simmer over very low heat for about 10 minutes. Meanwhile, boil the reserved cooking liquid to reduce somewhat; adjust the seasoning, if desired.

Serve the partridges on a mound of lentils, and pour some of the cooking liquid over each portion.

Serves 4.

Braised Partridge with Lentils. Don't hesitate to prepare this dish with chicken.

Herb-Simmered Partridge with Pasta

This simple dish is distinguished by the pasta, which is cooked in the broth.

4   partridges, 12 ounces each, halved
    Salt and freshly ground pepper to
    taste
2   tablespoons butter
2   tablespoons olive oil
1   clove garlic, chopped
2   tablespoons chopped fresh parsley,
    more for garnish
1   tablespoon fresh thyme leaves
1   cup dry white wine
3   cups chicken stock
1   onion, peeled and chopped
½   pound vermicelli

Season partridges with salt and pepper as desired. Heat half the butter and oil in a flameproof casserole over medium heat and brown the birds, in batches if necessary, on all sides. Add the garlic, herbs, wine, and one cup of stock. Cover and simmer over low heat until the birds are nearly tender, about 40 minutes.

Heat the remaining butter and oil in a skillet. Sauté the onion in it until wilted, then add the vermicelli. Cook, stirring constantly, until the noodles turn light brown. Butter a baking dish large enough to hold the partridges in one layer (or use two dishes). Spread the noodles in the bottom, arranging the birds on top of them. Add the remaining stock to the cooking liquid, bring to a boil, and season with pepper, if desired, then pour it all into the baking dish. Bake in a 425°F oven until the noodles are tender, 10 to 15 minutes. Sprinkle with parsley and serve.

Serves 4.

Cook birds and vermicelli together in wine for Herb-Simmered Partridge with Pasta.

Ring-neck pheasant is a native of Asia; it has been familiar in Europe since Roman times and was introduced to the United States late in the nineteenth century. Male pheasants have beautiful rusty plumage with a brilliant green ring at the neck; the hens have muted coloring. They are now indigenous and abundant in many areas and will often visit rural homeowners who have scattered cracked corn for them. Pheasants are also farmed commercially in the United States and some parts of Europe. Farmed pheasants have a milder flavor than wild ones, but in general pheasant meat is sweet and light with a texture similar to turkey; pheasant may be lean and need barding. Though pheasant is found infrequently on menus in the United States, it is quite common in Europe and many cooks consider it the most delicious game bird.

Pheasant, like chicken, should be prepared according to its age. When you purchase it, it is usually marked baby (one pound), adult (two to two-and-a-half pounds), or mature (up to four-and-a-half pounds). The younger pheasants are the most tender, can be roasted or grilled, and are delicious served cold as well as hot; mature pheasants should be braised or stewed. Allow about one pound, or one whole baby pheasant per person. *Smoked pheasant* is available from specialty food shops.

HOW TO ROAST A WHOLE PHEASANT

Refer to *How to Stuff and Truss a Bird*, page 106, *How to Bard*, page 108, and *How to Roast a Whole Bird*, page 108. Preheat the oven to 450°F, place the bird in it, and reduce the temperature to 350°F. Roast for 20 minutes a pound unstuffed, 25 minutes a pound stuffed, but check early for doneness. Allow a pheasant to rest about 10 minutes before carving.

RECIPES

Pheasant with Vinegar

This piquant braise is a nice complement to the sweet pheasant.

1	*tablespoon butter*
2	*tablespoons olive oil*
2	*2½-pound pheasants or* **1** *3½-pound pheasant, quartered*
4	*cloves garlic, peeled*
⅔	*cup herbal vinegar*
⅔	*cup dry white wine*
2	*ripe tomatoes, peeled, seeded, and chopped*
2	*teaspoons Dijon mustard Salt and freshly ground pepper to taste*

Heat the butter and oil in flameproof casserole over medium heat. Add the pheasant and garlic and cook until golden, about 10 minutes (do this in batches if necessary). Add the vinegar and cook until it evaporates. Add the wine and the tomatoes. Cover and cook over low heat until the pheasant is tender, about 60 to 75 minutes. Transfer the pheasant to a serving platter and keep warm. Puree the cooking liquid, or force through a sieve, and return to the pan. Stir in the mustard and simmer for a few minutes. Season with salt and pepper as desired. Spoon the sauce over the pheasant and serve.

Serves 4.

Pheasant with Vinegar.

Pheasant Salad with Shrimp, Melon, and Pasta

A pale and elegant salad for the hottest weather. Serve this on pale greens mixed with a few sprigs of watercress.

For the salad:
¼	pound macaroni or other medium-size pasta shape
1	tablespoon mild vegetable oil
1	medium honeydew melon
2	cups cooked pheasant meat, skin discarded
2	cups cooked medium shrimp, peeled and deveined
1½	cups finely sliced celery, preferably inner ribs

For the dressing:
6	tablespoons yogurt
2	tablespoons cream
2	teaspoons chopped fresh fennel leaves
1	tablespoon fresh lime juice
1	teaspoon gin
	Sugar to taste

Cook the pasta in boiling water until al dente; drain, rinse under cold water, and drain again. Transfer to a serving bowl and toss with the oil.

With a melon baller, cut about 2 cups of balls from the honeydew. Mix into the pasta with all of the remaining salad ingredients.

Mix all of the dressing ingredients except the sugar together in a small bowl. Sweeten if desired. Toss into the salad. Cover and chill for at least one hour before serving.

Serves 4 to 6.

Herb Braised Pheasant with Creamy Sauce

First a marinade and then gentle simmering suffuse both bird and braising liquid with herbal essence. Then the braised vegetables are pureed and mixed with sour cream to sauce the meat. Serve with baked or oven-roasted potatoes.

For the marinade:
1	onion, sliced
1	bay leaf, crumbled
6	sprigs thyme
3	sprigs rosemary
3	sprigs fennel leaves
2	tablespoons olive oil
⅔	cup dry white wine
2	2½-pound pheasants or **1** 3½-pound pheasant, quartered

For the braise:
3	tablespoons olive oil or butter
2	leeks, white parts only, cleaned and sliced
2	carrots, scrubbed and sliced
1	stalk celery, sliced
1	rib fennel bulb, sliced
	Salt and freshly ground pepper to taste
2	cups stock
3	sprigs thyme
2	sprigs rosemary

For the sauce:
2	teaspoons flour
1	cup sour cream
	Parsley for garnish

Mix the marinade ingredients together. Place the pheasants in a bowl or pan and pour the marinade over them. Cover and refrigerate for at least 8 hours; baste from time to time.

Lift the birds from the marinade, strain, and reserve it. Heat the oil in a deep, flameproof casserole and brown the birds on all sides. Remove from the casserole, lower the heat, and sauté the vegetables for about 5 minutes. Season with salt and pepper, if desired.

Mix the stock with the reserved marinade. Place the pheasants on their sides on the vegetables in the casserole and tuck the herbs around them. Pour the stock over them. Cover and simmer over low heat for 60 to 75 minutes, or until tender, turning the birds from time to time.

When done, remove the birds from the casserole and cut into serving pieces, if desired. Arrange on a serving platter. Cover and place in a warm oven.

Discard the herbs from the cooking liquid. Puree it in a food processor or force through a sieve. Place in a saucepan over medium heat. Do not let it boil. In a small bowl, whisk the flour into the sour cream until smooth, and slowly whisk into the pureed sauce. Cook gently for about 3 minutes, stirring constantly; adjust the seasonings. Pour the sauce over the pheasants on the platter and garnish with fresh parsley. If there is additional sauce, pass it separately to drizzle over potatoes or other side dish.

Serves 3 to 4.

When the weather is hot, serve Pheasant Salad with Shrimp, Melon, and Pasta.

Roast Pheasant with Peach and Walnut Sauce

The almost-sweet taste of the pheasant is enhanced by this faintly spiced fresh fruit sauce. If you happen to grow hyssop, put several sprigs of it in the birds' cavities with the lemon.

For the sauce:

4	to **5** *peaches*
½	*cup water*
2	*cardamom pods*
2	*teaspoons balsamic vinegar*
1	*tablespoon cognac*
1	*tablespoon honey*
1	*teaspoon butter*
⅛	*teaspoon ground cardamom*
¼	*cup walnuts, broken into small pieces*
2	*pheasants, about 2½ pounds each*
	Freshly ground pepper to taste
1	*lemon*
	Barding fat

Make the sauce at least four hours before you plan to serve it; you can keep it for a couple of weeks in the refrigerator. Peel the peaches (boil for 3 minutes if the skins are difficult to remove) and cut them into small pieces. Place in a small saucepan with the water and cardamom pods. Bring to a boil, cover, and simmer for about 20 minutes, stirring frequently. The mixture should be chunky and fairly thick; if it is watery, remove the cover and continue to simmer until it is somewhat reduced. Remove from the heat, remove the cardamom pods, and stir in all the remaining ingredients. Set aside.

Refer to *How to Roast a Whole Pheasant*, page 78. Season the pheasants with the pepper. Quarter the lemon and put 2 pieces in the cavity of each bird. Truss and bard the pheasants and place them on a rack in a roasting pan. Place in the oven and roast for 10 minutes; lower the heat to 350°F and continue to cook until done, about 50 minutes, or until the juices run clear. Baste from time to time and remove the barding fat for the last 20 minutes so the birds can brown.

Remove the trussing strings and halve, quarter, or carve the birds as you wish. Spoon a little of the hot peach sauce over each serving and pass the rest separately.

Serves 4 to 5; makes 1 cup of sauce.

Roast Pheasant with Peach and Walnut Sauce. Pheasant has a wonderful flavor that needs little or no enhancement; when you garnish the simply cooked bird with this conserve you can savor its true flavor while enjoying the complementary spiced fruit.

Quail are very small upland game birds. There are different varieties indigenous to Europe, Asia, North America, and Australia. Some quail are farmed and are available fresh year round. Quail can have either light or dark flesh, depending upon the breed. Some more commonly available types are the Bobwhite quail, which has light meat and lives wild in Texas, where it is also farmed, and the Courternix, which has dark meat and is farmed in Georgia and California. Quail usually weigh five or six ounces, though there is some variation due to breed or age.

Quail have a delicate flavor and are very lean, so take care not to let them dry out when cooking. They can be broiled, roasted, or fried and do not need very much seasoning; they are often served slightly rare. Because they are so tiny, they cook quite quickly, and look either very charming or somewhat disturbing when served—depending on your stomach for miniatures.

Frozen quail is often carried by better grocers. Specialty grocers and mail-order sources often offer it semi-deboned for a very small additional charge, which makes it easier to eat. *Smoked quail* is available from specialty shops. Allow two quail per person.

HOW TO ROAST WHOLE QUAIL

Refer to *How to Stuff and Truss a Bird*, page 106, *How to Bard*, page 108, and *How to Roast a Whole Bird*, page 108. Preheat the oven to 450°F, place the bird in it, and reduce the temperature to 350°F. Roast for 20 minutes unstuffed, or 25 minutes stuffed, but check early for doneness. Because they are so small, quail roast very quickly, and different recipes suggest various times. If not stuffed, you can roast them at a high heat (425°F) for about 8 minutes, and they will probably be perfectly done. You can also roast them for about 5 minutes at 400°F and then for 15 minutes at 300°F. They are delicate, though, so be sure not to let them dry out.

RECIPES

Pecan-Crusted Quail

Quail are raised in Texas, as are pecans; so it is fitting to combine the two for a twist on a traditional batter-crusted bake. You can deep- or pan-fry these if you prefer.

2 cups pecans
½ cup all-purpose or oat flour
½ teaspoon baking powder
1 egg
1 cup milk
8 quail, semi-deboned and butterflied
4 tablespoons melted butter

Run the pecans through a hand-grinder or chop very fine; mix with the flour and baking powder in a shallow bowl or pie plate. In another bowl, beat the egg with the milk. Brush a baking pan large enough to hold the quail in one layer with a little of the melted butter. Dip each quail in the egg, then dredge in the pecan-flour mix, and place skin-side up in the pan. Drizzle with the rest of the butter and place in 425°F oven. Reduce the heat to 350°F and bake for 20 minutes.

Serves 4.

Pecan-Crusted Quail.

Quail with White Wine and Shallots

Here is a very simple yet elegantly flavored way to prepare these birds. Serve them on toast if you like.

For the marinade:
- **2** tablespoons fresh rosemary leaves, coarsely chopped
- **16** juniper berries
- **⅔** cup dry white wine
- **3** tablespoons olive oil

For the quail:
- **8** quail
  Salt and freshly ground pepper to taste
- **4** to **6** tablespoons butter, more if necessary
- **8** shallots, peeled and sliced
- **½** cup dry white wine
- **1** teaspoon fresh rosemary leaves

Place the rosemary and juniper berries in the smallest possible saucepan. Barely cover with a little wine. Bring to a boil, cover, remove from heat, and let steep for ten minutes to release the flavors. Add the remaining wine and the olive oil and whisk to mix.

Place the quail in a shallow pan and pour the marinade over them, turning them to coat well. Cover the pan and refrigerate at least 8 hours.

When ready to cook the quail, remove them from the marinade, strain, and reserve it. Season the birds with salt and pepper, if desired, and truss them. Melt 4 tablespoons of the butter in an oven-proof skillet or sauté pan large enough to hold all of the birds and brown them

Quail with White Wine and Shallots served on a bed of new potatoes and finely shredded cabbage.

on all sides. Remove them from the pan and keep warm. Sauté the shallots in the butter until they wilt and turn transparent. Add more butter to the pan if necessary and return the birds to it. Cook them over a medium heat for about 10 minutes, turning them once. Add the wine and rosemary and place the pan in a 375°F oven to finish cooking, about 10 to 15 minutes more, or until the juices from the cavities run clear.

When the quail are done, transfer them to a platter and keep warm. Place the pan back on a medium flame and stir in the marinade. Bring it to a boil and simmer for a minute or two to thicken slightly. Pour over the quail and serve at once.

Makes 4 servings.

Mustard-Thyme Grilled Quail

Serve these tangy treats with couscous or millet, turnip slices cooked al dente, and a garnish of watercress.

For the marinade:
- **4** tablespoons whole-grain mustard
- **2** tablespoons cider vinegar
- **4** large shallots, minced
- **2** tablespoons honey
- **1** medium onion, finely chopped
- **¼** cup dry white wine
- **1** teaspoon chopped fresh thyme leaves

- **12** quail, split with breastbone removed

Combine all the marinade ingredients in a large bowl and mix to blend. Add the quail and turn to coat. Cover the bowl and refrigerate at least 8 hours, turning birds occasionally.

Brush the hot grill with oil. Grill the quail for 8 to 10 minutes per side, or until juices run clear when a skewer is inserted into the flesh; oil grill again when turning.

Makes 6 servings.

Quail with Raisin-and-Almond Sauce

The raisins give this sauce a sweet touch that complements the quail. You can grill rather than roast them, if you prefer. Serve on basmati rice.

For the sauce:
1   cup white wine, more if needed
    Juice of ½ lemon
2   tablespoons olive oil
4   tablespoons butter, more if needed
2   tablespoons all-purpose flour
¼   teaspoon nutmeg
1   tablespoon currants
3   tablespoons raisins, preferably golden
4   tablespoons slivered blanched
    almonds
    Salt and freshly ground pepper to taste

8   quail
2   lemons, quartered

Mix the wine with the lemon juice and olive oil in a large bowl, add the quail, and turn to coat. Cover and refrigerate at least 8 hours, turning occasionally. Drain the marinade from the birds and reserve; add more wine to make 1¼ cups if necessary. Place a lemon quarter in each bird and then truss; place in a baking dish.

Quail with Raisin-and-Almond Sauce—lightly sweet and spicy with a slight crunch.

SQUABS/PIGEONS/
DOVES

Melt the butter in a saucepan. Brush a little of the butter over the quail.

Begin the sauce. Stir the flour into the melted butter and cook over medium heat, stirring constantly, until it is smooth and golden. Stir in the nutmeg, then slowly stir in the wine marinade. When the sauce is smooth, stir in the currants and raisins; let the sauce simmer, stirring occasionally, while you cook the quail.

Roast the quail in a 400°F oven for 5 minutes, lower the temperature to 300°F, and continue to roast for 15 to 20 minutes. Baste them with pan juices occasionally; if there are none, use a little butter.

When the birds are nearly done, stir the almonds into the sauce and correct the seasoning. Serve the quail on a bed of basmati rice; drizzle some of the sauce over them and pass the rest separately.

Serves 4.

Pigeons and doves may be either farmed or wild; the Europeans have been raising them for centuries, and dovecotes or *colombiers* were once standard outbuildings at farms and country estates. *Squabs* are young pigeons (about four weeks old) that cannot fly because they do not yet have all their feathers. They are particularly tender and have more meat than you might expect, which is dark and richly flavored. Older wild pigeons and doves can be a bit tough and should be braised, but squabs can be prepared by any method and are so moist and tasty that they need little seasoning. Those that are truly wild have darker flesh and stronger flavor than those that are farmed; some hunters prefer their doves cooked medium rare. Frozen squab is sometimes carried by better grocers. Specialty grocers and mail-order sources often offer it semi-deboned for a very small additional charge, which makes it easier to eat. Pigeons and doves are not widely available at retail. Allow one to two squabs or doves, or one pound, per person.

HOW TO ROAST A WHOLE SQUAB

Refer to *How to Stuff and Truss a Bird*, page 106, *How to Bard*, page 108, and *How to Roast a Whole Bird*, page 108. Preheat the oven to 450°F, place the bird in it, and reduce the temperature to 350°F. Roast for 35 to 40 minutes unstuffed, or 45 to 50 minutes stuffed, but check early for doneness. If you prefer, you can roast the squab at 450°F for 5 minutes and then reduce the heat to 400°F and cook for 20 to 25 minutes more. Be sure to baste frequently. Let rest for 5 minutes before serving. Unless you are sure they are very young, wild doves and pigeons are best braised.

Plain fettuccine balances the rich birds in Brandied Squab on Pasta.

RECIPES

Brandied Squab on Pasta

Rich-flavored squab are delicious on a bed of pasta, and this dish can be prepared very quickly.

2	tablespoons butter
2	tablespoons olive oil, plus a little to toss through cooked pasta
2	small onions, peeled and sliced lengthwise
4	squab, halved and semi-deboned if possible, with their giblets
½	cup brandy
2	small sprigs rosemary
1	cup stock
1	pound lasagnette or other medium-width pasta
	Salt and freshly ground pepper to taste
	Grated Parmesan cheese for garnish

Heat the butter and oil over medium heat in a sauté pan large enough to hold all the birds. Sauté the onions in it until soft and golden. Add the squab, raise the heat, and brown for about 5 minutes on both sides. Add the giblets, brandy, and one sprig of rosemary. Cook uncovered until the liquid is reduced by half. Meanwhile, heat the stock in a saucepan. Add the hot stock to sauté pan, and season with salt and pepper, if desired. Cover loosely with parchment (or use an unfolded Chemex-type coffee filter) and simmer until squab is done, about 25 minutes. The sauce should reduce by about one-third; if it does not, remove the cover for the last 7 minutes of cooking. Cut the leaves from the remaining rosemary sprig and chop.

Meanwhile, cook the pasta until al dente. Drain and transfer to a serving platter, then toss with a little oil. Discard the rosemary sprig from the cooked squab. Remove the squab from the pan with a slotted spoon and keep warm. Add the cooking liquid, the chopped rosemary, and about 2 tablespoons Parmesan to the pasta; toss well. Top with the squab and giblets. Pass the Parmesan after serving.

Serves 4.

Squab with Red Wine

Here is a wine sauce with a piquant twist to counter the rich flavor of the squab.

4	squab, halved and semi-deboned if possible
3	tablespoons olive oil
	Grated rind of 2 lemons
2	tablespoons chopped parsley
4	sage leaves, chopped
3	tablespoons capers, rinsed, drained, and chopped
6	anchovy filets, chopped
½	cup dry red wine
	Freshly ground pepper to taste

Heat the oil in a flameproof casserole over medium-high heat, add the lemon rind and squab, and brown for 5 minutes on each side. Add herbs, capers, and anchovies and cook, stirring constantly, for 2 minutes. Stir in the wine, cover tightly, and simmer over low heat until tender, 20 to 30 minutes.

Serves 4.

Anchovies and capers lend piquancy to Squab with Red Wine.

Thyme-Poached Squab

This robust dish is particularly nice on a dank, chilly evening. It can be prepared ahead of time and reheated in a covered casserole. Use as many kinds of culinary thyme as you can—lemon thyme imparts a particularly good flavor.

> Sprigs of assorted fresh thyme, at least enough to fill a measuring cup loosely
> ¼ cup finely chopped chives
> 1 cup red wine
> 2 tablespoons olive oil or butter
> 4 squab, halved, with their giblets if possible
> Salt and freshly ground pepper to taste

Pull or cut the leaves from the thyme sprigs and add with the chives to the red wine; pour over the squab and giblets and let marinate if time permits.

Heat the oil in a sauté pan. Lift the squab from the wine, and brown for about 5 minutes on each side. Season with the salt and pepper, if desired. Add the wine with the giblets to the pan. Cover loosely with parchment (or use an unfolded Chemex-type coffee filter) and simmer until done, about 25 minutes more.

Serves 4.

Thyme-Poached Squab is hearty by virtue of the bird's inherently big flavor, not through the addition of rich ingredients. It is served here with wild rice, green beans, and pearl onions.

TURKEY

The turkey, golden, juicy, stuffed, and roasted, is the bird of choice on many holiday tables. A roasting turkey will fill the air with an evocative fragrance and then sate any number of appetites. The largest of the domesticated birds, turkeys are native to the Western Hemisphere. Recently discovered fossils indicate that they are a very ancient bird and were roaming the Americas as long as 10 million years ago. No one is sure when they were first domesticated, but there is evidence that they were confined by Indians in the Southwestern United States at least two thousand years ago; some experts believe that they were first raised by the Aztecs. Turkeys were taken to Europe by both Columbus and Cortez and were domesticated there by the mid-sixteenth century. Settlers who came to the New World in the early seventeenth century were familiar with raising and eating them before they arrived.

Turkey is delicious, economical, and nutritious. Though a turkey, depending on its size, will feed from eight to twenty people—far more than most of us usually serve—it is as good the second day as the first and there are many, many things to do with the leftovers. Indeed, for many people a real roast turkey sandwich is the ultimate lunch. Today turkey is available in a variety of sizes and cuts, so it is easier to prepare smaller amounts than once was true. Whole turkey is most often roasted; smaller cuts can be grilled, braised, or sautéed. Leftovers can be reheated, casseroled, or used in salads and sandwiches. The carcass can be boiled for soup. Turkey breasts and wings are white meat; thighs and drumsticks are dark meat. The meat—fresh or leftover—is very good sautéed in a little butter and can be served that way instead of bacon. Allow three-quarters to one pound per serving when buying a whole bird, or one-third to one-half pound boneless cut.

Domesticated turkeys have been bred to have a high proportion of meat to frame and to be particularly juicy and tender. The natural color of their plumage has been bred out, leaving them with white feathers; this was done because the fluid pigments in the feathers tend to leak out and stain the skin when the birds are plucked. As a result of the breeding processes, turkeys have lost some of the agility and cunning of their wild counterparts. Domesticated turkeys cannot fly.

Wild turkeys, on the other hand, can fly for short distances at a speed of 55 miles per hour; they can run at half that speed. Hunters consider wild turkeys to be great sport and they are being enthusiastically reintroduced to the wilderness in many parts of the United States. The Wild Turkey Federation works to preserve their habitats from development and to keep their numbers plentiful. Wild turkey can be prepared in any way that domesticated turkey can, but are leaner, so extra care should be taken not to overcook them—allow about 20 percent less cooking time. Also, as with any wild fowl, they use their legs, so the drumsticks may be tough and sinewy.

WHAT TO LOOK FOR IN THE MARKET

Turkey is available in many forms in most grocery stores. Whole or half *turkey breast* is available with and without the bone. Other bone-in cuts available are the *hindquarters* (thigh and drumstick); *drumsticks*; *thighs*; *wings*; *drummettes*, which are the first joint of the wing and serve as a white-meat "drumstick" to some; *flat wings*, with the first joint removed; and *necks*, which are good to boil for stock. Other boneless cuts available are *cutlets*, which are about ¼ inch thick and cut at an angle across the grain of the breast; *steaks* (or *tenderloins*), which are ½ to ¾ inch thick, respectively, and cut perpendicular to the grain of the breast; and *drumstick steaks*. These are all quite easy to cut yourself; it is also easy to remove the bone from a turkey thigh. *Ground turkey* contains both white and dark meat. *Smoked turkey* is available at some delicatessens and specialty food shops; it is very good in sandwiches and salads.

HOW TO ROAST A WHOLE TURKEY

Refer to *How to Stuff and Truss a Bird*, page 106, and *How to Roast a Whole Bird*, page 108. Plan to check turkey for doneness about an hour before you expect it to be ready and periodically after that. Preheat the oven to 450°F, place the bird in it, and reduce the temperature to 350°F. Roast for 15 minutes a pound unstuffed, or 20 minutes a pound stuffed. Let the roast turkey rest about 20 minutes before carving.

COOKING TIMES FOR VARIOUS CUTS OF TURKEY

Turkey is widely available in assorted cuts. These can be cooked in most of the ways appropriate to chicken, as long as you adjust the cooking time to reflect the larger size of the pieces. The meat is done if the juices run clear when a skewer is inserted into the flesh. Take care not to overcook turkey.

Here are a few guidelines:

To cook bone-in parts: You can use a meat thermometer if you wish; insert it into the thickest part of the flesh without touching a bone and cook until it registers 170°F for white meat, 180°F for dark. Bake bone-in wings, thighs, and drumsticks at 325°F for 1 to 1¾ hours; breasts as you would a whole turkey: Place in 425°F oven and immediately lower the heat to 350°F, bake for 15 to 20 minutes a pound. If you are cooking turkey parts *uncovered*, check them from time to time and baste to keep from drying out; do this even if there is sauce in the pan.

To pound to make thin: Place steaks or cutlets between wax paper and pound with a wooden mallet or side of a rolling pin. If you plan to roll and stuff them, be careful not to pound holes into the flesh.

To broil steaks or tenderloins: Pound to flatten; marinate if desired. Brush the grill or broiler rack with butter or oil, arrange the steaks on it, brush them with butter or oil, and broil 5 to 6 inches from the heat for 5 to 7 minutes on a side for steaks, 8 to 12 minutes for tenderloins. Brush with butter or oil after turning.

To bake steaks or tenderloins: Marinate if desired. Brush with butter or oil, place in one layer in a shallow pan, season as desired, cover pan, and bake in a 400°F oven for 20 to 30 minutes.

To cook cutlets: Brush with butter or oil and seasoning if desired; grill, broil, or sauté for 2 to 3 minutes per side.

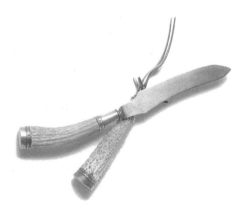

RECIPES

Turkey and Spinach Phyllo Rolls

These are a lovely party-food; double the recipe and make the rolls larger to serve 4. Phyllo pastry sheets are available frozen in many groceries; otherwise check a specialty food retailer.

2   tablespoons olive oil
1   small onion, finely chopped
3   large cloves garlic, pressed
½   pound ground turkey
½   teaspoon hot red pepper flakes
     Salt and freshly ground pepper to taste
1   10-ounce package frozen chopped spinach, thawed and drained
1   cup feta or farmer cheese
½   pound phyllo pastry sheets
½   cup melted butter, or as needed

Heat the oil in a skillet over high heat, add the onion and cook, stirring, until transparent, about 3 minutes. Add the garlic and cook 30 seconds. Add the turkey, breaking it up with a fork, and sauté until cooked through, 5 to 8 minutes. Season with the salt and peppers.

Remove from the heat. Stir in the spinach and cheese, mixing until well blended. Adjust the seasonings if desired. Cool to room temperature.

Cut the phyllo into strips about 4 × 5 inches. Work with one strip at a time, keeping the others covered with plastic wrap to prevent drying out. Brush strip with melted butter. Place about 2 teaspoons turkey mixture at one end, fold up once, then fold in sides and roll up. Brush all sides with melted butter and place on a cookie sheet. Repeat until all filling is used.

Bake at 450°F until golden brown, about 15 minutes. Cool slightly and serve warm.

Serves 16 to 20 as an appetizer.

A WORD ON GROUND CHICKEN AND TURKEY

Contemporary nutritional wisdom indicates that we should all be cutting down on the amount of fat we eat. Poultry producers are now packaging ground chicken and turkey so that there is a versatile lower-fat alternative to ground beef. These cuts are quick and easy to prepare, but there are a few things to consider before you cook them.

Ground poultry *is* low in fat. It tends to be drier than ground beef and does not have the same juicy consistency; it does not shrink as much during cooking either. Brush it with oil or use a non-stick pan when grilling or sautéing.

Ground poultry tastes like whichever bird it is. It doesn't taste like hamburger. When you plan to cook it, think of seasoning it as you would any other cut of chicken or turkey—with herbs, onions, apples, vegetables, wine, soy sauce, or vinegar; ketchup may not be the most complementary choice. One of the advantages of any ground meat is that seasonings are easily blended with it, suffusing it with their flavor, so think of enhancing ground poultry in its own right rather than using it as a direct beef substitute. If you want inspiration for experiments, look to ethnic recipes for ground lamb, which are traditionally seasoned with fruits, spices, and herbs, and think of serving ground poultry with a sauce, as you might meatballs. If you wish to substitute ground poultry for beef in your favorite lasagna or meatloaf recipe, consider adjusting the seasonings and be prepared for results that are not as juicy as the original.

Day-After-the-Feast Soup

Once the meat has been eaten (or otherwise removed from the frame) a turkey carcass retains enough flavor to make a wonderful pot of soup. Put this on to simmer early in the day so that it can cool, allowing the fat to solidify on the surface for easy removal; then reheat with the diced vegetables.

Note: If your turkey was smaller or larger than indicated, adjust the amounts of the other ingredients.

For the soup base:

1	turkey carcass (14 pounds originally)
1	bay leaf
2	teaspoons fresh or 1 teaspoon dried each rosemary and thyme
6	to **8** juniper berries
4	peppercorns
2	whole onions
2	cloves garlic
3	carrots
3	stalks celery, with leaves
½	medium turnip, cut into 2 to 4 pieces
3	quarts cold water, or as needed

To finish:

½	medium turnip, diced
1	boiling potato, diced
1	to **2** leeks, white parts only, thinly sliced
2	carrots, thinly sliced
2	stalks celery, thinly sliced Salt and freshly ground pepper to taste
1	cup fresh or frozen green peas
½	cup chopped parsley

Cut any turkey meat from the carcass and reserve to add to the finished soup. Tie the bay leaf, rosemary, thyme, juniper berries, and peppercorns into a piece of cheesecloth. Place all of the ingredients except the water in a large stockpot; break up the carcass, if necessary, so that it fits efficiently in the pot; cut the vegetables in half if need be. Then pour in cold water to almost cover. Bring slowly to a boil, uncovered, then cover and simmer over the lowest possible flame, turning the bones once or twice, for 1½ to 2 hours, or until the bones are clean. (You can add more water if evaporation is extreme, which happens when the flame is too high.)

Remove from the heat and let stand, covered, until cool enough to handle. Lift the bones, meat, and vegetables from the pot and let drain in a sieve over the stockpot so as to retain the liquid, then discard them. Strain the liquid in the pan. Refrigerate for several hours, then lift the fat from the surface.

Cut reserved turkey into bite-size pieces. Shortly before serving, reheat the soup. Add the potato, turnip, and leeks, and simmer, covered, for about 7 minutes. Add the carrots, celery, and turkey, and simmer 5 minutes. Season with salt and pepper as desired, add the peas, breaking them up if frozen, and cook 2 minutes more. Serve garnished with parsley.

Makes about 3 quarts.

Turkey Burgers

Cook these on a grill if possible and serve with a crusty peasant bread. Garnish with fresh tomato slices if in season, or sun-dried .omatoes dressed with a little olive oil if not.

1	pound ground turkey
3	large shallots, peeled and chopped Grated rind of 1 lemon
2	teaspoons herbes de Provence
3	tablespoons balsamic vinegar Salt and freshly ground pepper to taste Olive oil

Mix all ingredients except olive oil. Cover and refrigerate for 2 hours or overnight. Shape into patties and drizzle with olive oil. Brush the grill or pan with oil; cook 5 to 6 minutes on a side or until juices run clear when poked with a fork.

Serves 3 to 4.

As it simmers slowly on the stovetop, Day-After-the-Feast Soup smells almost as good as the roasting bird.

Smoked Turkey and Pasta Salad

This salad can be served warm or at room temperature. It makes a great luncheon or buffet dish.

¼	pound dried small pasta shapes
4	tablespoons olive oil
½	pound smoked turkey, flaked into 1½ to 2-inch pieces
¼	cup thinly sliced button mushrooms
4	teaspoons fresh chives, coarsely chopped
	Freshly ground black pepper
1	teaspoon balsamic vinegar
1	large or **2** small avocados, quartered and sliced
⅓	pound smoked mozzarella, cut into ½-inch cubes

Cook the pasta, rinse in cold water, drain well, and set aside.

Heat 3 tablespoons of the olive oil in a large skillet and add the turkey, mushrooms, and chives; season with pepper and sauté quickly until turkey is lightly browned. Add the vinegar and 1 tablespoon of oil and cook, stirring constantly, until the juices are thickened and reduced. Season with more pepper. Add the pasta, toss to mix, and cook 15 seconds.

Remove the pan from the heat and mix in the avocado and cheese, stirring well to distribute the heat. Let the dish rest for 2 to 3 minutes or cool to room temperature before serving.

Serves 4.

Smoked Turkey and Pasta Salad.

Basic Ground-Turkey Kibbe

Inspired by the Middle Eastern classic usually made with ground lamb, this versatile mixture can be shaped into patties or balls, used as a stuffing for vegetables (a recipe for stuffed zucchini follows) or pastry, or wrapped around skewers; grill, pan-fry, or simmer in sauce as desired. Serve with rice or pita bread, and accompany with minted yogurt sauce. Depending on how you prepare it, it can be an appetizer or main course.

For the kibbe:

4   *tablespoons olive oil*
1   *small onion, peeled and chopped*
2   *cloves garlic, or more to taste*
½   *cup cooked chick-peas*
2   *tablespoons chopped fresh coriander leaves*
2   *tablespoons chopped fresh mint leaves*
½   *lemon*
2   *tablespoons plain yogurt*
1   *pound ground turkey*
     Salt and freshly ground pepper as desired

For the yogurt sauce:

1   *cup plain yogurt*
1   *tablespoon chopped fresh coriander leaves*
1   *tablespoon chopped fresh mint leaves*
     Juice of ½ lemon
     Salt and freshly ground pepper as desired

Heat 1 tablespoon of the oil in a skillet and sauté the onion over medium heat until soft and transparent. Do not brown. Squeeze the garlic through a press over the pan so as not to lose any of the juice, and stir into the onion. Add another tablespoon of oil to the pan along with the chick-peas and cook for five minutes, stirring frequently. Stir in the herbs. Transfer to the container of a food processor. Squeeze the lemon into the hot skillet and deglaze (scrape any remaining bits into the juice), add to the mixture in the food processor, and puree. (If you do not have a food processor, force the mixture through a sieve or food mill.) If the mixture is still hot, let it cool in the processor. Add the yogurt, the remaining oil, the turkey (¼ pound at a time), and the salt and pepper; puree until well blended.

Shape the mixture as desired and cook appropriately—5 to 6 minutes on a side for patties, less for balls or skewers. Avoid overcooking.

To make the sauce, mix all the ingredients together. Serve chilled or at room temperature, or drizzle over kibbe-stuffed vegetables for the last 5 minutes of baking.

Serves 3 to 4.

Variation:

Turkey-kibbe stuffed zucchini: Slice 4 to 5 young zucchini in half lengthwise and scoop out the flesh; discard or reserve for another use. Place the shells in a shallow baking pan in one layer, drizzle with a little olive oil and chopped coriander, and add a small amount of water to the pan (just enough to cover the bottom). Cover and bake in a 350°F oven for 10 to 15 minutes, until they begin to soften. Remove from the pan and discard any liquid. Fill each zucchini half with the turkey mixture, and dot with raisins if desired. Return to the pan, and cover and bake for about 20 minutes. Spoon the yogurt sauce over each zucchini and bake, uncovered, for another 5 minutes.

Turkey Kibbe kebobs are a leaner variation on their lamb counterparts.

Rolled Stuffed Turkey Breast

This is a pretty and festive way to prepare a boneless turkey breast. Two very different filling recipes are offered; make your own bread crumbs from good white bread if possible.

Pesto filling:

3	cups bread crumbs (unseasoned)
1	egg, lightly beaten
3	cloves garlic, minced
⅔	cup grated Parmesan cheese
1	cup finely chopped basil leaves
½	cup pine nuts or chopped walnuts
	Freshly ground pepper
6	tablespoons olive oil or melted butter, or as needed

Raisin, apple, and ginger filling:

3	cups bread crumbs (unseasoned)
1	egg, lightly beaten
1	tart apple, cored and chopped
¼	cup raisins
4	inches fresh ginger root, peeled and grated
½	teaspoon cinnamon
1	pear, cored and chopped
2	to **3** tablespoons honey
8	tablespoons butter, or as needed

For the turkey:

1	4½-to-5-pound turkey breast, halved, bone removed but skin remaining
½	cup water
2	tablespoons oil or melted butter

To make the pesto filling, mix all of the ingredients except the olive oil or butter in a large bowl, then add as much of the oil or butter as needed to moisten. To make the raisin filling, mix all of the in-

Roast Turkey is inexpensive and easy to prepare, and the leftovers are as good as the first meal. Any of the fillings on these two pages can be used to stuff a whole bird.

gredients except the honey and butter in a large bowl. Melt the honey with 4 tablespoons butter and add, tossing to mix and moisten; melt additional butter if necessary.

Lay the turkey breast halves skin-side down on a large board covered with wax paper. Slice them horizontally almost all the way through and open out flat. Cover with another piece of wax paper and pound to flatten slightly.

Spread the desired filling on the turkey breast halves, then, beginning with the non-skin section, roll up jelly-roll style; secure with toothpicks or tie with string. Place the rolls on a rack in a roasting pan. Add water to the pan. Brush the rolls with the oil or melted butter. Bake uncovered in a 350°F oven for ½ hour, then cover with foil and bake for another 45 minutes. Let stand covered for 15 minutes before slicing.

Serves 10; makes about 5 cups of each filling.

Basic Bread Stuffing

There are probably as many ways to season turkey stuffing as there are people to make it. This is a basic recipe that you can use as is, or alter as suggested, or as inspiration strikes. Don't hesitate to begin with different kinds of bread (it need not be stale). Remember that oysters, nuts, and sausage make a stuffing rich and that vegetables will not stay crisp—which may or may not be to your liking—and do not use raw pork. It is traditional, but not necessary, to add one or two beaten eggs to bread stuffing to help it stick together.

Note: Refer to *How to Stuff and Truss a Bird*, page 106, and *How to Roast a Whole Bird*, page 108.

8	*cups cubed bread*
1	*cup minced onion*
1	*cup chopped celery*
1	*apple, cored and chopped*
2	*to **4** tablespoons fresh herbs of choice, assorted if desired: thyme, tarragon, rosemary, fennel, basil, oregano, dill, parsley*
½	*cup stock or water, heated with*
¼	*cup butter*
	Salt and freshly ground pepper to taste

Spread the bread cubes on a cookie sheet and dry in a 300°F oven for 15 to 20 minutes. Do not brown. Combine all the ingredients in a large bowl and toss to mix well.

Makes enough to stuff a 12- to 14-pound turkey.

Variations:

• Sauté the onion in butter before adding.
• Add 1 to 2 cups of other chopped fresh and dried fruit such as pears, apricots, raisins, lemons (with the peel), cranberries, or cubed winter squash; season with mint and/or spices such as cinnamon, cloves, nutmeg, and cardamom instead of herbs.
• Add 12 to 18 chestnuts: To peel chestnuts easily, place them in a small saucepan and cover with water. Bring to a boil, then remove the pan from the heat. Using a slotted spoon, remove the nuts one at a time and, with a paring knife, peel off both the shell and the inner skin. Discard any flesh that is moldy; cut the chestnuts into small pieces.

• Add 2 cups nuts: Brazil, hazel, walnut, pecan, almond, pine; toast first in a shallow pan in a 350°F oven for 15 to 20 minutes (5 to 7 minutes for pine nuts), if desired.
• Use alliums other than onions: leeks, shallots, or garlic as appropriate to the bird and the menu.
• Add 1 to 2 cups mushrooms: Use the familiar button type or try some of the more exotic imported and dried varieties; sauté first, if desired.
• Add 1 to 2 cups shredded cabbage; season with caraway seeds.
• Add 1 to 2 cups bacon or ham with the mushrooms or cabbage.
• Add 2 cups oysters; delete the apple and use milk instead of stock to moisten mixture.
• Add 2 cups browned sausage or pork or chicken livers.
• Moisten mix with brandy, sherry, wine, or liqueur.

Turkey Braise

Here is a hearty, warming, and inexpensive stew.

6 to **7** pounds turkey thighs, or thighs and drumsticks (4 to 5 pieces)
2 onions, peeled and chopped
4 cloves garlic, peeled and minced
1 tablespoon herbes de Provence
1 cup white wine, optional
3 cups stock
4 plum tomatoes, coarsely chopped
3 medium potatoes, peeled and quartered
3 carrots, cut into ¾-inch chunks
1 turnip, peeled and cut into 1-inch chunks
1½ cups fresh or **1** package frozen baby lima beans
2 teaspoons fresh or **1** teaspoon dried thyme
Salt and freshly ground pepper to taste

Place the turkey parts skin-side up in a flameproof casserole and bake uncovered in a 450°F oven for 25 minutes, until skin is brown. Remove the turkey and discard all but 2 tablespoons of the fat from the pan. (Remove the skin from the turkey at this point, if desired.) Heat the pan over a medium flame and sauté the onions and garlic in the remaining fat. Add the turkey and the wine, if using; cook over high heat till it evaporates. Add the stock, the tomatoes, and the herbs. Reduce the heat, cover, and simmer until the turkey is nearly tender, about ½ hour. Add the potatoes, carrots, and turnip. Cover and cook until tender, about 20 minutes.

Turkey Braise—a basic recipe that you can easily adapt to suit your imagination and your local vegetable market.

Transfer the vegetables and turkey to another pan and keep warm; remove the meat from the bones and cut into bite-size pieces, if desired. Skim any excessive fat from the pan juices. Add the lima beans to the pan, breaking them up if frozen. Cover and cook quickly until almost done. Stir in the thyme; season with salt and pepper to taste. Return the turkey and vegetables to the pan and heat through.

Serves 7 to 8.

Turkey Tetrazzini

A classic for leftovers.

4 tablespoons butter
1 onion, peeled and chopped
1 small red pepper, cored and chopped
1 small green pepper, cored and chopped
½ pound button mushrooms, cleaned and chopped
2 cloves garlic, peeled and crushed
4 teaspoons fresh thyme leaves
¼ cup flour
2½ cups stock
1¼ cups milk
¼ cup dry sherry or white wine
Salt and freshly ground pepper to taste
2½ cups cooked shell noodles
3½ to **4** cups cooked turkey meat, cut in bite-size pieces
⅓ cup grated Parmesan cheese
1¼ cups bread crumbs

Melt the butter in a large saucepan, add the onion and peppers, and cook, stirring, over medium heat until tender. Add the mushrooms, garlic, and thyme and cook, stirring, for 2 minutes. Stir in the flour and cook 1 minute.

Mix the stock, milk, and sherry and add slowly to other ingredients; cook, stirring constantly, until mixture has boiled and thickened. Season with salt and pepper.

Add the noodles and turkey, stir to mix, and pour into a casserole. Mix the Parmesan and bread crumbs, sprinkle on top and bake in a 350°F oven for 30 minutes or until golden brown.

Serves 6.

Grilled Turkey Breast with Scallion-Dill Butter

This dish can be pulled together in minutes. Serve it with potato salad, fresh peas, and some very crisp red radishes.

4	*turkey breast steaks (about 1½ pounds), pounded to ¼-inch thickness*
2	*tablespoons olive oil*
2	*large shallots, minced*
	Salt and freshly ground pepper to taste
4	*tablespoons butter*
	Juice of ½ lemon
4	*tablespoons minced fresh dill*
1	*scallion, sliced very thin*

Place the turkey steaks on a piece of wax paper. Brush both sides with olive oil and sprinkle with the shallots. Season with salt and pepper.

In a small saucepan, melt the butter over low heat; stir in the other ingredients and mix well. Cover and keep warm.

Grill the turkey steaks for 2 minutes on each side, or until done. Place on a serving plate and drizzle with the butter.

Serves 4.

Grilled Turkey Breast with Scallion-Dill Butter is a quick dish that offers instant gratification. Experiment with other herbs, and don't hesitate to use this recipe with other birds—or with fish or lamb for that matter.

APPENDIX

HOW TO CUT UP, BONE, AND SKIN A BIRD

The most economical way to purchase chicken or turkey is whole, and many of the other birds are available only that way. It is a simple matter to cut them up for baking, braising, or grilling. All of the birds may be handled in the same way, though it is not usual to cut the smaller ones into sections less than halves, and a large turkey will be awkward to cut up yourself. Be sure to use a firm, sharp knife, and/or poultry shears.

Before you remove the bones from a bird, consider how you will be preparing and serving it. Bones add flavor to any recipe, so it may not be an advantage to remove them, but bone-in poultry will not cook as quickly as boneless. Many recipes can be prepared with the bones in or out as long as you adjust the cooking time. If you are concerned about your fat consumption, then be good to yourself and remove the skin before cooking; you probably won't miss it if it isn't there and it is hard to ignore that wonderful golden crispiness once on the plate.

TO CUT A BIRD INTO NINE PIECES

1. Place the bird, breast-side up, on a cutting board. Cut the skin between the thighs and the body.

2. Grasping one leg in each hand, lift the bird and bend back the legs until the bones break at the hip joints.

3. Remove the leg-thigh pieces from the body by cutting from the tail toward the shoulder between the joints, close to the bones in the back.

4. Separate each thigh and drumstick; place skin-side down on the board, locate the knee joint by bending the thigh and leg together, then cut through the joint.

5. With the bird still on its back, remove each wing by cutting inside of the wing just over the joint, then pull the wing away from the body and cut from the top down through the joint. If desired, cut the tips (and second joints) from the wings so they will be more attractive—this is particularly nice if you are serving chicken wings as hors d'oeuvres.

6. Separate the breast from the back; place the bird on the neck-end and, holding the tail section, cut diagonally

A bird cut into nine pieces.

toward the board through the joints along each side of the rib cage.

7. Place the breast skin-side down and cut through the wishbone and the cartilage at the neck end of the breastbone. Bend the breast back to pop the bone, loosen the flesh with your fingers, and pull or cut the bone from the breast. Cut the breast in half. Some people cut the back crosswise in half; many simply save it to make stock.

TO HALVE OR QUARTER A BIRD

1. Place the bird on its back, then cut from the neck to the tail end through the breastbone.

2. Pull the two sections apart to break the ribs away from the backbone, then cut out the backbone.

3. If quarters are desired, cut each half into two sections; place skin-side up and cut between the thigh and the breast along the rib cage.

A bird being quartered.

TO BUTTERFLY A BIRD

Butterflying splits a bird open without cutting it completely in two. It is a nice preparation for smaller birds, particularly if they are to be grilled.

Place the bird breast-side down on a board. Cut through all the bones along one side of the backbone, repeat along the other side, and discard the backbone. Spread the two sections apart. Cut through the wishbone and the cartilage at the neck end of the breastbone. Bend the breast back to pop the bone, loosen the flesh with your fingers, and pull or cut the bone from the breast. Flatten the bird out with your hands.

Above: A butterflied bird. Loosely stuff a bird (right) and truss with pins (opposite page, left) or with heavy cotton thread (opposite page, center and right).

TO REMOVE THE RIB CAGE

You can easily cut the rib cage from a butterflied, halved, or quartered bird, or a breast.

Place the piece skin-side down, insert the tip of the knife under the long rib bone inside the thin membrane, and slice it free from the flesh. Working from the wishbone end, slide the knife between the ribs and flesh and cut free.

TO REMOVE THE SKIN

Once a bird is cut up, it is quite easy to remove the skin from everything but the wing tips. With your fingers, gently pull the skin away from the flesh and use a small sharp knife to cut the membrane that joins them. Use the knife to cut through the skin around the end of each drumstick and at the wing joints so that it can be pulled free. Cut away any fatty deposits.

HOW TO STUFF AND TRUSS A BIRD

Stuffings both enhance and absorb the flavor of a roast bird. When planning a stuffing, allow about ¾ cup for every pound of bird; if this does not seem like enough to go around, make more and bake it separately in a covered casserole, basting with some of the pan juices. You may prepare stuffing ahead of time, but to prevent the growth of bacteria, always store it separately until roasting time. Even if both the bird and stuffing are chilled when you put them together, the

cold of the refrigerator may not fully penetrate a stuffed bird. (Should you buy a prestuffed bird from your grocer, be sure to cook it the day of purchase and do not freeze it uncooked.)

You can also stuff a bird with whole or large pieces of fruits or vegetables and herbs that lend flavor but may or may not be eaten. Onions, apples, and citrus fruits are frequent choices.

If you remove the wishbone before roasting a bird, it will be easier to carve the breast meat. Place the bird on its back and slide back the skin around the neck cavity. Locate the wishbone with your fingers. Starting at the top, use a small sharp knife to cut along the sides of the bone, freeing it from the flesh. Slip your finger into the arch of the bone and pull it out.

If desired, season the cavity of the bird with salt and pepper before preparing it for roasting. When stuffing a bird, never fill the cavities more than three-

quarters full. Stuffing expands during roasting and an overstuffed bird may split; this is particularly true of small, deboned game birds. If roasting a large bird such as a turkey or goose, stuff the neck cavity first, closing it temporarily with a skewer, then stuff the body cavity.

If you like, you can stuff a bird under the breast skin. Loosen the skin around the openings and gently lift it to separate it from the breast. Fill this pocket with a moist stuffing (one that has been pureed will be easiest to handle). Again, do not overstuff, so that the skin will not rupture during roasting. With larger birds, you can slit the breast meat while holding back the skin, and insert seasonings such as herbs, garlic slivers, citrus peel, or nuts into the meat. It is traditional to slip softened butter under the breast skin, but that seems inappropriate to today's health-conscious cuisine and is necessary only for lean game birds that require barding (see page 108).

Whether a bird is stuffed or not, it should be trussed before it is roasted. Trussing closes the cavities and secures the wings and legs close to the body. It improves the appearance of the cooked bird and makes it easier to handle and to turn if desired. More importantly, it assures that the smaller parts will cook at the same pace as the rest of the bird. Remove the trussing before you bring the bird to the table.

You can truss a bird with heavy cotton thread and a darning needle or skewers and twine. For very small birds, toothpicks may be used. First, with the bird on its back, close the body cavity: either lace twine over skewers placed across it or sew through the skin with the needle and thread; catch the tail toward the cavity as you do this. Then tie the drumsticks together with the twine (if you are trussing a short-legged bird, there will be an inch or so between them). Turn the bird over and tie another length of

twine around the neck skin, then pass the ends of the twine under the top joint of the wings and tie the twine over them to secure. Fold the wing tips onto the back so they sit akimbo.

If you are trussing a chicken or similar-size bird, you can do it entirely with twine: Cut a 4-foot length of twine, place the bird on its back, and place the middle of the twine under the tail. Wrap each end of the twine around one leg, crisscross it over the cavity and under the legs to the sides, pulling tight; turn the bird over, pass the twine along the breast and loop it around the upper joint of each wing, fold the neck skin to the back, and tie the ends of the twine over it securely. Cut any excess twine. Fold the wing tips onto the back so they sit akimbo.

Ducks and geese have very high breastbones. To keep these from browning too quickly, hit them with a mallet before trussing to flatten.

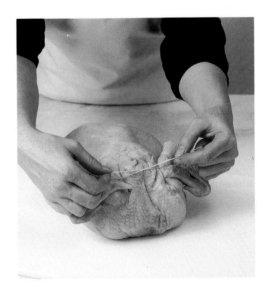
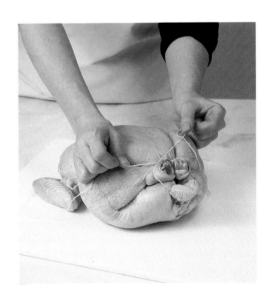

Tuck barding material between the legs and the body of the bird.

Wrap barding material around breast and legs of the bird.

Tie barding material in place with heavy cotton thread.

HOW TO BARD

Most game birds are very lean and their meat will be quite dry if they are simply roasted in their skins. To prevent this, they should be covered with bacon or ¼-inch-thick slices of salt pork after they are trussed: Slip a piece of barding fat between each leg and the body, then cover the legs and breast with additional pieces (bear in mind that the fat shrinks as it cooks); tie the fat in place with kitchen twine wrapped around the bird. If desired, remove the fat when roasting is nearly complete (half an hour before for larger birds, ten to fifteen minutes for smaller ones) so that they can brown. Bacon can be served with the bird if you like, but salt pork should be discarded.

Both bacon and salt pork tend to be very salty, so you may wish to blanch them before using: Slice as appropriate, place them in cold water, bring to a boil, and simmer for 2 to 3 minutes. Drain, place in cold water to firm, and drain again. If you do not blanch them, you will not need to use any additional salt.

You can also bard a bird under the skin. Loosen the skin around the open-

ings and gently lift it to separate it from the breast. Fill this pocket with butter, or a paste of butter and/or olive oil and crushed herbs. As you roast the bird, baste it with any drippings.

If you do not want to use a fatty meat to bard a bird, you can wrap it in several layers of grape leaves, steamed cabbage leaves, or even romaine lettuce; this method is not true roasting as it adds a little steam to the cooking process, but it is considerably less fatty or salty. Soak the leaves in wine, vinegar, or hot water for about half an hour, drizzle the bird with a little olive or other vegetable oil, and then wrap with the leaves, tying them on with kitchen string. Drizzle again with oil before roasting. (If the bird is small like quail, partridge, or Cornish game hens, you can simply bury it in a blanket of leaves.) To impart a seared flavor to the bird, brown it on all sides in a little butter or oil before you wrap it. Or, if you wish the bird to brown at the end of the roasting time, remove the leaves as you would the barding fat. In either case, discard them before serving.

HOW TO ROAST A WHOLE BIRD

Only young birds should be roasted; older ones should be cooked with a moist heat—braised or stewed. You can judge the age of domestic poultry by understanding the labeling system used, but with game birds you probably have to go by weight. In either case, refer to the specific chapters for guidelines. Most game birds available commercially are farmed and therefore "of the year" or young enough to roast; hunters know the signs of age for the different species shot in the wild.

DOMESTIC POULTRY

Once a bird has been trussed (see page 106), roasting it is a fairly simple matter. The only real trick is to know when it is done. Small birds can be roasted resting on the bottom of a pan, but for best results place them on a lightly greased flat or V-shaped rack. Large birds and fatty birds should always be roasted on a V-shaped rack. Domestic duck and goose should be handled somewhat differently from other poultry (see below).

Roasting is by definition a dry-heat process in which the skin and outer flesh cook quickly, sealing in the juices, which transmit the heat to the interior. Do not cover a roasting bird with foil or it will steam and seem stewed; removing the foil for the final half hour of roasting to "brown" the bird may dry out the meat. To ensure that a bird browns properly, roast it uncovered, basting frequently; if it browns before it is done, then cover it loosely with foil. Another method that works well with a larger bird is to cover it with a cotton or linen cloth half an hour after it goes in the oven. (Doubled cheesecloth is fine, as you will have to discard the cloth when through.) Be sure the edges of the cloth are inside the pan. Baste through the cloth as soon as you put it on and then as you would normally; then remove it for the last half hour of roasting. Some cooks recommend that the cloth be presoaked in unsalted shortening, but the pan drippings work just as well and have the flavor of the bird. This method has other advantages: It keeps the breast meat moist while the dark meat cooks through, requires less frequent basting, and diminishes splattering.

The most successful roasting occurs when the (room-temperature) bird is placed in an oven preheated to 450°F and the temperature is immediately reduced to 350°F. This seals in the flavor. In general, birds weighing two to six pounds should be roasted for 20 minutes a pound unstuffed; birds over six pounds for 15 minutes a pound unstuffed. However, very small birds such as Cornish Game Hens may require 30

to 40 minutes per pound to be cooked through and large ones like turkey may surprise you by being ready an hour before you expect them to be. Increase the roasting time by 5 minutes per pound if the bird is stuffed.

In truth, predicting roasting time is an inexact "science," and there are almost as many rules governing it as there are cooks. Though it makes mealtime a bit uncertain, you should be prepared for variation from bird to bird and oven to oven—even the type of pan you use can affect roasting time. The important thing is that a bird should be neither overcooked (which makes it dry) or undercooked (which is not healthy). There are signs indicating doneness that you can learn to recognize: If a bird is properly cooked, the juices that run from the cavity when it is tipped off the rack, or from a fork or skewer inserted into the thigh, should be clear. If they are pink, the bird is not done. It is often said that if the drumstick wiggles easily the bird is ready, but this may not happen until the breast meat is beginning to dry out. If you want the reassurance of a more scientific technique, insert a meat thermometer between the thigh and body before putting the bird in the oven, being sure that the tip does not touch the bone. Poultry should be cooked to an internal temperature of 185° to 190°F.

There are differing views as to whether a bird should be turned as it roasts. Certainly it is not necessary, but turning it allows all sides to brown. There are people who insist that a turkey that is first roasted breast down will be juicier than one that is roasted entirely breast up, but a large, hot bird is difficult, if not dangerous, to turn. Cer-

tainly all birds may be cooked and rotated on a spit, but this is usually done outdoors, unless one has an electric rotisserie.

If you wish to glaze a bird, do so during the last half hour of roasting. At this point you can dust it with flour, let the flour set, and then baste through it. Alternately you can brush the bird with a glaze made from honey or preserves and melted butter, using one of the recipes for glazed birds in this book or one of your own.

DOMESTIC DUCKS AND GEESE

These birds are naturally quite fatty and should be handled a little differently so that their excess fat cooks off as they roast. They can be stuffed just as any other bird can be, but be aware that the stuffing will absorb some of the fat and be rich. (Some people recommend that goose and duck be partially cooked before they are stuffed to minimize this.)

After trussing a duck or goose, prick its skin a few times all over, but not its meat, so that the fat can drain. Place it in a rack in a pan that is at least 2 inches deep so that it can hold the drained fat. To help the fat drain quickly, you can cook a duck or goose at a higher temperature—450°F for duck, 400°F for goose—for one third to one half of its roasting time and then lower the temperature—350°F for duck, 325°F for goose—for the remainder. From time to time prick the skin again and remove the excess fat from the roasting pan with a bulb syringe or large spoon; be very careful when doing this because the fat will be very hot. If the bird is small enough to turn easily, cook it for a while on each side and the fat will drain more efficiently.

GAME BIRDS

Game birds (including wild ducks and geese) are lean and almost always require barding before they are roasted. They can be roasted following directions for comparably sized domestic birds (see above), but they are often roasted at 400° or 450°F for some or all of their cooking time, so refer to individual recipes. Many of them are traditionally served on the rare side, but only experimentation can tell you if this is your preference.

HOW TO CARVE

While small roasted birds may be served whole or simply cut in half, large ones must be carved. Be sure to let the bird rest before carving, as indicated in the individual chapters, otherwise the flesh may shred rather than slice cleanly.

Place the bird breast up on a platter or carving board, and have another warm platter ready to hold the meat. Use a long, flexible, and sharp knife, and a two-tined carving fork. To look like a pro, hold each slice after cutting between the knife and the fork to transfer to the platter. To keep the flesh from drying out, cut from only one side of a large bird at a time, and do not carve more than you need. If you did not remove the wishbone before roasting, you may do so before carving.

Turkey, capon, chicken, guinea fowl, and pheasant can all be carved by the same method, though with the smaller of these, the flesh is not usually cut from the drumstick or thigh. Duck and goose are carved somewhat differently because their carcasses are of a different shape.

CARVING A TURKEY-LIKE BIRD

1. With your left hand, pull one leg away from the body. Sever the hip joint with the knife point to remove the leg

(below, left). Slice the dark meat from the body above the joint, following the contour with the knife.

Lay the leg flat and separate the drumstick from the thigh by cutting through the joint.

2. Hold the drumstick (by the foot end) upright or at a slight angle and slice the meat from it, cutting down (below, center).

Use the fork to steady the thigh and, cutting parallel to the bone, slice the meat from it.

3. Insert the fork in the breast, flatten out the wing with your hand or the knife, and cut diagonally down between the wing and breast to sever the joint (below, right).

4. Hold the back of the fork against the breastbone on the side of the breast you are carving, and with the tip of the knife toward the tail end, slice diagonally down through the meat (opposite page, left).

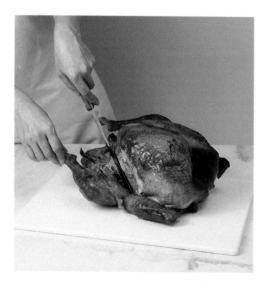
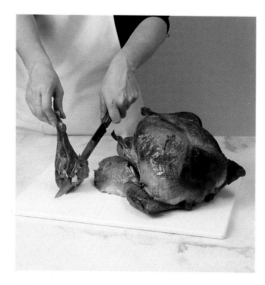
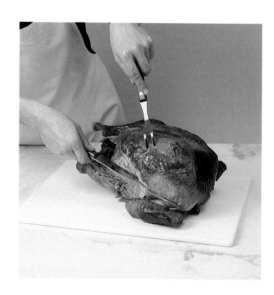

TO CARVE A GOOSE

Because the ligaments of a goose are heavy, you will need a rigid knife to cut through them, as well as a flexible one to carve the meat. Do not serve the fatty skin around the neck cavity and trim any excess fat from the meat as you carve.

1. Wiggle the wing to locate the shoulder joint, insert the rigid knife between wing and breast, and sever the joint.

2. Cut an arc in the skin around the leg and press the knife between the leg and body to expose the joint, which is farther under on goose than it is on turkey. Sever the joint, then separate the drumstick from the thigh as you would for turkey.

3. Hold the back of the fork against the breastbone on the side of the breast you are carving and the tip of the flexible knife toward the neck end, and slice diagonally down through the meat.

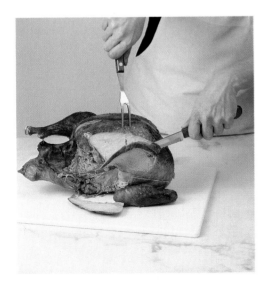

TO CARVE A DUCK

Before carving, lay the duck breast-side down and pull the neck skin away from the body. Cut it off in one piece. Turn the duck breast-side up to carve. As with a goose, you will probably need a rigid knife to sever the joints, and should trim any excess fat as you carve.

1. Wiggle the wing to locate the shoulder joint, insert the rigid knife between wing and breast, and sever the joint.

2. Slice along the center line of the breast, cutting through the skin and flesh to the bone.

3. Slide the knife between the bone and the flesh on one side of the breast and carefully free the meat from the rib cage, slicing through the skin to separate it at the lower edge.

4. Pull the leg down and away from the carcass to expose the joint and sever the joint, but leave the thigh and drumstick as one portion.

Repeat these steps to carve the other side of the duck. If you like, cut the carcass into two pieces crosswise, but unless someone wants to pick at the bones, this part is perhaps better saved for stock.

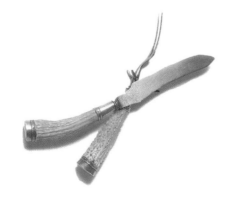

HOW TO GRILL OR BROIL

Unless you have a commercial range, you will probably find it difficult to satisfactorily broil poultry—other than cutlets—indoors. It is impossible to regulate the heat in the broiler of most domestic stoves or to get the pan far enough from the flame to prevent burning; besides, broiling can make an awful mess. If you do wish to broil, remember that it is a dry-heat cooking method that works best for small or flat pieces of meat that will cook quickly. Be sure to preheat the broiler and grease the rack lightly.

Outdoor grilling, on the other hand, is a wonderful way to cook poultry and game birds. Follow the manufacturer's directions to prepare your grill; when building a fire remember that poultry should be thoroughly cooked, so the coals must be both hot and mellow enough to give an even heat throughout the cooking time. For best results grill poultry by the indirect method: Arrange the hot coals on the perimeter of the grill and place a disposable pan or piece of foil under the middle of the rack, then place the poultry over it; this pan will catch the fat and keep it from flaming up and charring the meat. Be sure to allow the rack to preheat, and grease it lightly before placing the meat on it. For most recipes it is your choice whether or not to cover the grill, but doing so intensifies the smoky flavor and helps keep the heat even.

If you have a large, covered grill and add coals to the fire every hour to maintain the heat, you can cook a whole turkey or duck in it; smaller birds can easily be grilled whole if desired. In either case, be sure to bard if appropriate and truss them. Do not stuff large birds that you plan to grill whole. For the most part, though, it is probably most satisfactory to butterfly (split along the back, remove backbone and breastbone) or cut the bird into halves or smaller pieces so that it can cook quickly in the dry heat. If you split a bird, it is quite easy to then remove the backbone and breastbone, which will allow it to lie flat on the grill and cook evenly. If you also remove the rib cage, it will be easier to eat. Poultry can be skinned before it is grilled; however, there is some evidence that charcoal grilling, like so many other things, is not healthful. If poultry is grilled skin-side down and the skin discarded before serving, the ill effects of the charcoal may be minimized.

Cooking times vary greatly with the size and cut of the meat and the type of grill; do refer to the manufacturer's handbook and trust your previous experience where possible. Here are some guidelines for cooking by the indirect method: Whole or large bone-in cuts of turkey or capon can take as much as 75 minutes per pound; it is a good idea to use a meat thermometer with these. For large boneless cuts, allow about 30 minutes per pound. For domestic duckling and roasting chickens, allow about 2 to 2½ hours per bird, 1½ to 2 hours if split or quartered. Allow 1½ to 2 hours for a whole broiler or comparably sized game bird, 1 to 1½ hours if split or quartered. If a grilled bird is done, the juices will run clear when a skewer is inserted into the flesh. White meat will cook more quickly than dark, so if you are grilling quarters, you can give it somewhat less

time. You can half-cook whole birds or bone-in cuts in the microwave or conventional oven to cut down on grilling time; do not let them stand but transfer to the hot grill immediately to finish cooking.

Cooking time for boneless breasts (other than whole turkey breasts), cutlets, steaks, and burgers is considerably less and depends upon the thickness of the cut; these cuts can be grilled directly over the coals. Very thin (¼-inch cutlets) may require only 3 to 4 minutes per side, thicker cuts 7 to 10 minutes per side, and burgers 6 to 7 minutes per side.

Whether you broil or grill, marinating the meat first will help to protect it from drying out, as well as enhance the flavor. If you like, you can glaze the bird with barbecue sauce or a sweet- or fruit-based glaze when it is nearly done.

Grilled poultry and game birds can be part of any summer-type menu, but they are particularly complemented by grilled vegetables and potatoes, and by grain salads—rice, bulgur, or wheat berry; if you do not think of these as a matter of course you might like to try them. In addition, most grilled birds are very good cold, or at room temperature, and can be used to make unusually flavorful salads—just be sure to discard any skin and fat that were not removed before cooking.

HOW TO BRAISE AND CASSEROLE

Braising and casseroling are slow, covered, moist-heat cooking methods that are ideal for older birds. The cover keeps steam from escaping from the

pan, so the juices given off by the bird are retained, and blends their flavors with whatever other liquid or seasonings are used. When a braise or casserole is done, the bird should be removed from the pan and kept warm while the cooking liquid is degreased or deglazed, and sauced and reduced if appropriate. Birds can be braised or casseroled whole or cut up; depending upon size and preference, they are very often sautéed till brown before being covered.

Technically, the difference between the two techniques lies in the amount of liquid used. Casseroling is usually done in the oven; braising often, but not always, on the stove top. To cook a bird in a casserole, place it in a heavy pan with a minimum of water or stock, and any seasonings desired, and bake in a 300°F oven for at least one and a half hours, or until the meat is tender. To braise, bring the stock or water to a boil in a separate saucepan, place the bird in a heavy pan, on a rack or bed of minced vegetables (onions, carrots, celery) if you like, and pour in the hot liquid to a depth of 1 to 2 inches (depending on whether or not the bird is cut up), but not deep enough to cover the meat. Cover the pan, bring to the boiling point, reduce the heat and simmer for at least one and a half hours, turning the bird occasionally.

You can add vegetables to either dish for flavor. However, a long cooking period is likely to make them mushy, so you may wish to discard them near the end of the cooking time and add fresh vegetables, cut in small pieces so they heat through quickly.

When the bird is cooked, remove it (and any vegetables) from the pan, and keep warm. Skim the fat from the pan. If you have prepared a casserole, deglaze the pan with a small amount of wine, stock, or water, scraping all the brown bits into the liquid to make a sauce, and reduce if necessary. If you have prepared a braise, strain any minced vegetables from the liquid and reduce and thicken it as desired; correct the seasoning once the sauce reaches the desired consistency. Depending upon the type of dish you are preparing, you may wish to return the meat to the pan or serve it from a platter.

HOW TO MAKE POULTRY OR WILD FOWL STOCK

Many recipes call for stock to be used as the cooking liquid because it will provide a more flavorful base than water. Canned stock or broth is readily available, but it tends to be very salty, as do bouillon cubes; if you must use it, it is a good idea to dilute it by half. But it is not at all difficult to make your own stock, which can then be frozen in ½-cup or ice-cube-size portions so as to be handy when needed. Stock will keep for 4 to 5 days in the refrigerator, and 3 months in the freezer.

Unlike much contemporary cooking, which prizes tender young ingredients quickly cooked to retain texture and vitamins, stock can be made from foods often discarded as being unpalatable or unappetizing—tough or tired vegetables or peelings and trimmings, and poultry parts—necks, backs, bones, and even feet. The cooking time is prolonged to obtain the optimum flavor. Once the simmering period is over, the stock is strained from the ingredients, which are discarded; it can then be further simmered to reduce it and thus intensify the flavor. If reduced far enough, it can even be used as a sauce.

The basic ingredients for poultry stock, in addition to poultry bones and water, are onions, carrots, and celery. Other vegetables and herbs and spices can be added as desired, but when doing so, consider how they will affect the flavor of the finished stock; if you are not making stock to use in a specific recipe, avoid strongly flavored additions such as garlic, coriander, or turnip that might compete with other ingredients. Poultry stock is commonly seasoned with bay leaf, an onion studded with a few cloves, and parsley or a little thyme or rosemary. Leeks will contribute wonderful flavor as well. You might like to add peppercorns to stock, but it is just as well to leave it unsalted as different recipes require such different amounts of salt, and reduction, storage, and the addition of wine all tend to intensify saltiness.

When making stock, allow about 1 quart of water for each pound of bones and parts; the yield will equal about half the liquid with which you begin. Water and all other ingredients should be cold; this will help to extract the juices. For best results, the poultry parts should be blanched to eliminate excess fat before beginning the stock. To do this, place them in a pan, cover with cold water, bring slowly to a boil uncovered, drain, and plunge in cold water. If you do not blanch them, begin the stock with just the parts and water, bring to a boil, and skim the surface before adding the remaining ingredients. The stock should be simmered uncovered, not boiled, so that it does not become bitter.

You can use a carcass instead of or in addition to bones, but it will not give as much flavor. If possible, remove any fat and skin from poultry parts or a carcass before adding to the pot. It is your choice to peel the vegetables or not.

If desired, the fat that rises to the surface when the finished stock is chilled can be refrigerated separately and used in place of butter or oil in appropriate recipes. It will keep for 2 to 3 months.

Poultry or Wild Fowl Stock

5	pounds poultry and/or wild fowl backs, necks, bones, and feet, blanched
5	quarts cold water
1	medium onion studded with 5 cloves
2	leeks, cleaned and chopped
1	medium onion, chopped
2	carrots, chopped
5	to 6 stalks of celery, with leaves, chopped
1	bay leaf
2	sprigs fresh or 1 teaspoon dried thyme
6	to 8 sprigs parsley

Place all ingredients in a stockpot and bring slowly to a boil, uncovered. Reduce the heat immediately and simmer for about 3 hours, or until reduced by half. Cool and strain. Refrigerate or freeze, and skim the fat that rises to the surface before using the stock.

Makes about 2½ quarts.

 # SOURCES FOR GAME AND SPECIALTY FOODS

D'Artagnan
399-419 St. Paul Avenue
Jersey City, NJ 07306
1-800-327-8246
Wild game and fowl, foie
gras, smoked game, and
duck fat.

Durham Night Bird
358A Shaw Road
South San Francisco, CA 94080
1-415-737-5873
Exotic produce, gourmet food
products, and wild game and
fowl.

Foggy Ridge Game Bird Farm
P.O. Box 211
Warren, ME 04864
1-207-273-2357
Range chicken, mallard,
guinea fowl, organic
ring-necked pheasant,
chukar partridge, bobwhite
quail, and wild turkey.

The Game Exchange
107 Quint Street
P.O. Box 880204
San Francisco, CA 94124
1-800-GAME USA or
1-415-647-1300
Wild game and fowl, exotic
produce, and imported
gourmet products.

Wild Game
2315 West Huron Street
Chicago, IL 60612
1-315-278-1661
Wild fowl, venison, buffalo,
smoked meat, poultry, and
fish, caviar, and gourmet
food products.

INDEX

SCHENECTADY COUNTY COMMUNITY COLLEGE

3 0313 00159 792 2

TX 750 .S685 1993

Spier, Carol

Food essentials

DATE DUE

SCHENECTADY COUNTY
COMMUNITY COLLEGE
LIBRARY